Being an Effective Progr
Higher Education

Being an Effective Programme Leader in Higher Education is a practical guide designed to help navigate the complex academic, pastoral, and administrative challenges that come with working in this position.

This book looks at topics such as leadership, personal tutoring, and academic and student support mechanisms from the unique perspective of the programme leader. It gives suggestions for effective ways to lead a programme, incorporates practical advice on some key leadership skills, and offers proven strategies from across various contexts within the role. Vignettes, which include descriptions of authentic situations provided by programme leaders, sit alongside probing questions to prompt reflection for professional development.

This practical text is a must-read for programme leaders working in higher education and provides the guidance necessary to help them create an environment that is inclusive, caring, compassionate, and supportive.

Sarah Naylor is a Diagnostic Radiographer who as a Senior Lecturer has been programme leader for undergraduate and postgraduate programmes at Sheffield Hallam University and the University of Derby.

Being an Effective Programme Leader in Higher Education

A Practical Guide

Sarah Naylor

LONDON AND NEW YORK

Cover image: Getty Images

First published 2023
by Routledge
4 Park Square, Milton Park, Abingdon, Oxon OX14 4RN

and by Routledge
605 Third Avenue, New York, NY 10158

Routledge is an imprint of the Taylor & Francis Group, an informa business

British Library Cataloguing-in-Publication Data
A catalogue record for this book is available from the British Library

Library of Congress Cataloging-in-Publication Data
Names: Naylor, Sarah, 1964- author.
Title: Being an effective programme leader in higher education : a practical guide / Sarah Naylor.
Description: Abingdon, Oxon ; New York, NY : Routledge, 2023. |
Includes bibliographical references and index.
Identifiers: LCCN 2022007403 (print) | LCCN 2022007404 (ebook) |
ISBN 9780367641863 (hardback) | ISBN 9780367648046 (paperback) |
ISBN 9781003126355 (ebook)
Subjects: LCSH: College administrators. | Educational leadership. |
Universities and colleges--Administration.
Classification: LCC LB2341 .N3854 2023 (print) | LCC LB2341 (ebook) |
DDC 378.1/11--dc23/eng/20220503
LC record available at https://lccn.loc.gov/2022007403
LC ebook record available at https://lccn.loc.gov/2022007404

ISBN: 978-0-367-64186-3 (hbk)
ISBN: 978-0-367-64804-6 (pbk)
ISBN: 978-1-003-12635-5 (ebk)

DOI: 10.4324/9781003126355

Typeset in Times New Roman
by Taylor & Francis Books

This book is dedicated to my amazing family past and present. Family always comes first.

Contents

Figures

Tables

Acknowledgements

I would like to thank my mentor and critical friend Ian Turner who has supported and encouraged me throughout the process of writing this book and donned his imaginary programme leader hat to provide feedback on the chapters. I am also grateful to my pool of critical friends Emma Hyde, Sarah Booth, Ian Baker, Uche Okere, and Ann Minton who have helped shape the chapters of this book.

The vignettes enhance this book and bring it to life. For these I have to thank the programme leaders who were willing to share their stories and experiences.

A big thanks and appreciation to my family and friends who support me and to my academic buddies Amelia Drake, Denise Foulkes, and Sarah Booth who believe in me.

Introduction

Programme leaders in higher education have considerable responsibility and a wide variety of roles to fulfil. Whilst universities produce guidance and handbooks for programme leaders, these primarily include what the role consists of and what they are required to do but with limited information about how these tasks can be achieved. In the ideal world programme leaders will have some lead into the role with mentoring and guidance available from more experienced academics. This is not always the case and lecturers can become overwhelmed by the enormity of the role. This book offers strategies that have worked in practice across various contexts within the role of programme leader.

The changing world of academia and increased commercialisation, with students being viewed as consumers, puts pressures on programme leaders. There is often demand for increasing student numbers and programmes are heavily monitored with pressure to be rated highly in a variety of league tables. This is a 'go-to' book for guidance on various aspects of leading a programme. The book looks at topics such as leadership, personal tutoring, and academic and student support mechanisms from the unique perspective of the programme leader. However, the information contained will not only be valuable to programme leaders but also module leaders and year tutors, especially new academics. The overall aim of this book is to provide guidance to help academics thrive in their roles.

Being an Effective Programme Leader in Higher Education is evidence-based, drawing on theory and using scenarios and questions interspersed throughout each chapter to prompt critical reflection on various aspects and challenges of the role. Vignettes from programme leaders talking about their experience act as reassurance that programme leaders, whatever the discipline, often encounter similar situations and experience similar feelings.

This Introduction provides an overview of the contents and rationale for the book. It also includes advice on how to use the vignettes and reflections critically in a way that will support your professional development.

The genesis of the book

This book is drawn from the experiences as a programme leader in a variety of programmes. My first programme leadership was for a collaborative

DOI: 10.4324/9781003126355-1

programme whilst I was still in clinical practice as a diagnostic radiographer. This was for a master's programme in mammography. On moving into higher education my first programme was for a master's programme. This was a programme which had a mixture of distance learning and face-to-face modules. Students could pick from a variety of modules to complete a bespoke programme. The challenge with leading this programme was the large number and diversity of students and being able to keep track of who was doing what and when. Most students were still in full-time employment undertaking a part-time degree. Monitoring the student experience was challenging. My next programme leadership was for a full-time undergraduate degree for a professional programme. This programme grew from about 35 students to 60 students over a few years. There was a marked difference in how I needed to lead and manage the programme as the numbers increased. For example, a strategy of having year tutors helped manage the student experience. My most recent experience of programme leadership is for a small full-time professional programme. With numbers averaging around 16 per cohort this is a nice programme to lead. However, I have been faced, along with other programme leaders, of leading a programme throughout the pandemic. In December 2020 I wrote a blog for Advance HE.

Juggling the virtual balls as a programme leader

Programme leaders have responsibility and accountability for their programmes. It is a challenging task at best as this juggling act is often fulfilled with no managerial responsibility over the people delivering on the programme. The plethora of roles a programme leader has to keep in the air at the same time can frequently feel like a ball may drop at any moment. It is a mammoth task at the best of times, but extremely challenging today. The way to survive and thrive in the role is through collaboration with the people connected with the programme: students, academics, administrative colleagues, student support, placement providers – and others could be added.

How do you maintain this connectivity when you can no longer meet people for a coffee and catch up, bump into people in the office or staff room, nip down to the administration office to ask a quick question? How can you be responsive to the frequent and sudden changes to delivery of a programme when you are working from a room in your home?

Connectivity and collaboration require effort, planning, and organisation. The virtual classroom does not lend itself to informal consultation and feedback from students before or after classroom delivery. In these rapidly changing times, gauging the feelings of students needs to be more frequent than the standard timed surveys. Connectivity and collaboration with students should be in a variety of ways. You can make yourself available by published programme leader drop-in sessions, setting up a virtual room for students to access. Take-up of these is likely to be minimal but they do make you visibly accessible. Regular programme student representative meetings are valuable for sharing and receiving information. Although you may only capture the most dominant voices, short regular meetings can help to iron out issues before they become a big problem. Scheduling time for an open 'coffee and chat' session allows any student to ask questions in an open forum, creating the opportunity not only for you as programme leader to respond but also facilitating the sharing of ideas from other students and peer support.

Along a similar line, connectivity and collaboration with other staff members leading or delivering modules will not just happen casually. Regular programme delivery meetings provide a platform for discussion about individual modules, allowing the opportunity for discussion about any issues. This not only keeps you informed as programme leader, but also facilitates collective solution finding. Whilst a programme leader does not have responsibility for staff, they are accountable for the delivery of the programme and therefore ensuring teaching sessions are covered. If people work in isolation on their modules this will be challenging. Therefore, promote a culture of openness and transparency. Make use of virtual document-sharing platforms and encourage the use of these. Documented session planning has never been more important to allow another member of staff to pick up and run a session at short notice.

A programme leader is frequently a sounding board for staff, students, and senior leaders in the institution. You are in a pivotal position and as a result can be expected to absorb additional work and pressure. It is vital for your own health and well-being not to be a recipient of this work and pressure but to be a conduit for it. Regular meetings with your line manager will make them aware of your current situation and facilitate a solution. Don't keep things to yourself thinking you have to cope; if people don't know, they cannot help. The programme delivery meetings with your team not only facilitate discussion about their issues but also give you a platform for sharing. Engaging with other programme leaders can be a great source of support. Some universities will be facilitating programme leaders' meetings; if not, reach out to those you know who are in a similar situation. Keep connected to your administrative and support staff. Emails are quick and documented but picking up the phone or, even better, holding a video call improves your connectivity and can be more productive than a series of emails.

In summary, it's good to talk. How are you facilitating this?

(Naylor, 2020)

Chapters

Here I provide a summary of each chapter. Chapter 1 provides an overview of approaches to leadership with reflections on successful strategies. Leadership is frequently associated and confused with management but effective leaders are not always good managers and vice versa. As a programme leader there is generally no managerial authority; consequently, in academic leadership personal qualities are important, as it is these and not the position that establishes an individual as credible for programme leadership. Theories associated with leadership are discussed and applied to programme leadership. The chapter includes practical suggestions on effective ways of leading the programme delivery team. It incorporates discussion and practical advice on some key leadership skills. A vignette provides the experiences of a programme leader applying their leadership skills. Questions are provided to prompt your reflection and assist your professional development.

Chapter 2 discusses your support mechanisms. Programme leaders have numerous, potentially conflicting roles to fulfil. The plethora of roles a programme leader has to keep in the air at the same time can sometimes feel like juggling and that a ball may drop at any moment. The main support available for programme leaders from various universities is information about the roles and responsibilities of programme leadership, of which there are many. Various programme leader courses do exist, some within institutions and others from external organisations. These generally cover curriculum design, learning and teaching approaches, organisation of a programme, and pedagogy. Peer support can be an invaluable mechanism which will help you fulfil your role as programme leader. There is value in sharing experiences with other programme leaders, as long as this is in a non-threatening environment. Moral support from colleagues can help you build self-confidence. Mentoring can also be a valuable source of support for programme leaders. This chapter provided ideas on how to get the most out of a mentoring relationship. Networking via programme leader forums can be a valuable source of support. This chapter acknowledges that programme leaders can be susceptible to workplace stress. This is exacerbated by increasing student number, widening participation, and the consumerist approach to higher education. Particularly with new ways of working the blurring of work and non-work in the lives of programme leaders is likely and can lead to work-related stress. This chapter discusses issues faced by programme leaders in terms of their well-being and support and provides strategies for being a healthy programme leader.

Chapter 3 talks about issues around quality. As a programme leader, you will have some accountability for the quality of your programme. This chapter looks at what quality in a programme means and how this is measured. To help achieve what is required it is useful to understand why certain policies and procedures are in place. To develop this understanding this chapter starts by looking at a historical view of quality assurance in higher education from the Thatcherite government changes in the 1980s to 2020. The chapter continues by discussing current quality assurance and concludes by providing strategies for quality improvement. Vignettes have been used to illustrate how programme leaders have approached the issue of quality in their programmes. Scenarios relating to quality improvement have been provided to prompt reflection on your programme.

Chapter 4 covers the design and approval of a programme. It focuses on approaches you can use when designing your programme. It starts by discussing your role in the process of programme validation and tips that you may find helpful for fulfilling your role. Engagement with stakeholders is an essential part of designing a programme. You are prompted to think about who this might be for your programme. Co-creation of your programme, particularly with students, will enhance your programme. This concept, along with practical guidance and questions, are included to aid your reflection of using co-creation to develop your curriculum. The involvement of other stakeholders from placement providers, employers, and people using their services all need to be involved in the development of a programme to ensure it is fit for its purpose. The second part of the chapter explores change management. Starting with curriculum justification and situation it is followed by techniques that you can use for consultation. Vignettes describe how programme leaders have used some of these techniques. The final part of the chapter explores some of the major themes you need to consider when developing your programme, including education for sustainable development, internationalising your curricular, and embedding employability skills.

Chapter 5 looks at a variety of issues impacting on the student experience. It starts with the mental health of students in higher education which is high on the agenda across the world and is something that should be considered by programme leaders who have an important role in the mental well-being of their students. Your programme should be challenging and at times may be stressful for your students. This chapter looks at how you can create an environment that is inclusive, caring, compassionate, and supportive. It discusses ways of embedding mental well-being into your curriculum and creating conditions that facilitate positive mental health by being active, learning, taking notice, connecting, and giving. Personal tutoring can impact on student experience and retention. This chapter includes ways that you can support this within your programme, ensuring each student can be signposted to the support they need. It also includes supportive peer relationships such as peer mentoring and peer tutoring which support your students and help develop employability skills. There are points for you to consider around the organisation of these initiatives such as the recruitment and training of mentors and peer tutors. With a now ethnically diverse body of students entering higher education, issues of equality, diversity, and inclusion are discussed within the role of a programme leader. The last section covers analytics. Students leave a data footprint throughout their interaction at university which can help you gain an understanding about your students' experience and be an asset in your role as programme leader.

Chapter 6 explores how you can enhance your students' experience through the introduction of external expertise. It identifies how external experts can contribute across the life cycle of your students and in doing so improve the quality of your programme. There are benefits to the students in terms of employability and benefits for the external experts such as in developing their curriculum vitae. There are challenges in engaging external expertise, and it takes organisation and management. You need to identify, recruit, and reward appropriate external experts. Both the external expert and students may need preparation and support to gain the most out of any interaction. Within this chapter there is discussion around involving external experts in admissions, curriculum delivery, and assessment

Chapter 7 is about facilitating students' learning through real work experience. This can take many different formats and comes under a variety of terminology; for example, internships, work-integrated learning, and placement. These may range from short projects to placement thoroughly integrated into your programme. Work-based learning within the context of higher education is programmes where the higher education providers and work organisations jointly create learning opportunities. Students on your programme are likely to require some work-based learning experience. As this is part of your programme you need to be aware of what it entails, how to support your students, and ensure that they have a quality learning experience. The chapter starts with an overview of work-based learning before looking at the work-based learning provider, managing the student experience, and quality. Degree apprenticeships are increasing and the final section in this chapter has provided a short overview of these. A vignette discusses an experience of a programme leader dealing with a difficult situation. Questions are used to prompt critical reflection on how you can optimise your student's work-based learning.

Vignettes

Vignettes within this book are descriptions of authentic situations provided by programme leaders. Vignettes have been used for many educational and research purposes. In this book vignettes have been provided in order to elicit discussion and initiate reflection. Critical thinking can be used to evaluate different aspects of the situations described and ultimately enable you to reflect on your practice. Vignettes can be used in different ways; the closest definition for how they have been utilised in this book is adapted from Jeffries and Maeder (2005):

> Short stories that are written to reflect real life situations in order to encourage discussion and prompt reflection.

Used in this way vignettes can trigger a learning process and aid professional development. Triggers can prompt you to explore a topic further, challenge your current thinking, and explore new ways of working. Learning in this way is situational, an active process that is bound within a specific context (Lave and Wenger, 1991). Vignettes combined with reflection can be a powerful tool for personal and professional development.

Reflection

Reflection is an essential part of professional development. Questions have been used within this book to prompt your reflection. Reflective practice is about learning from experience, both yours and that of others. It helps to make you more aware of your situation and to be able to see your practice through different lenses. There are many different strategies to reflection and tools that enable deeper reflection:

- Jenny Moon uses a series of questions to facilitate reflection and to prompt more profound reflection (Moon, 2013).
- Gibbs's reflective cycle has a six-stage approach enabling you to explore an experience, your associated feeling, and plan your development (Gibbs, 1988).
- David Kolb has a similar four-stage model prompting you to observe your experience, learn from it, and plan further experience (Kolb, 2014).
- Schon (2008) encourages you to reflect in action and reflect on action. He distinguishes between reflecting whilst actively engaged in a situation and a deeper reflection after the event.
- Driscoll's model of reflection is one of the simplest, but is a very effective model. This three-stage model encourages you to describe an event (what?) and explain any significance relating to the event (so what?), before explain how you will use the information (now what?). (Driscoll and Townsend, 2006)

Figure I.1 is a diagram depicting what you should think about when critically reflecting.

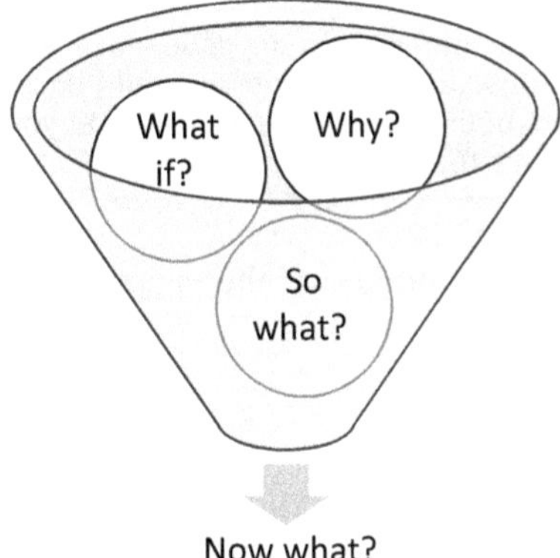

Figure I.1 Critical reflection

Here is an example of a reflection on a vignette:

> **Vignette**
> Remote working has made it really hard to connect and collaborate with both students and the teaching team. Students are starting to comment on the lack of face-to-face teaching and comparing the amount of time they have with students on other programmes. It is hard to balance student experience and safety. The decision was made by the university to have a blended approach to delivery, but the balance of face-to-face and virtual varies between programmes.

Reflection

Looking through the different lenses at this issue:

As a programme leader it is impossible to predict the future. It is therefore important to have a programme that is able to adapt the delivery of the programme to accommodate any restriction that may be in place in the future. Consultation with delivery staff and students is important so that there is a collaborative approach to planning. This can be challenging if face-to-face contact is restricted, but use can be made of remote team meetings and online polling.

The delivery team have their own opinions and concerns about face-to-face teaching. Many have become accustomed to remote working and adjusted family life accordingly. Each person is likely to have different ideas about how the programme should be delivered. They will want their concerns and ideas considered. There may be compromises made such as to the start and finish time of sessions to accommodate child care.

Students want value for money and some want the 'student experience'. They may not view remote delivery as being good value and feel that they are missing out. It is hard for them to gel as a cohort, make friends, and socialise with each other. There needs to be strong and regular consultation with students to clear up any misconceptions, and try to meet their expectations. Devise opportunities for collective learning experiences.

The university will be concerned about meeting the requirements of the Office for Students and quality measures such as the National Student Survey and Teaching Excellence Framework. Student satisfaction will be high on their agenda and the university is likely to produce guidelines for the delivery of programmes.

Now what?

Future plans should take into account any guidance from the university and plans made in consultation with staff and students. It would be useful to connect with other programme leaders both within the university and your sector to share ideas, current practices, and plans for the future.

The book ends with a summary of the chapters and supports you in the development of an action plan.

References

Driscoll, J. and Townsend, A., 2006. Alternative methods in clinical supervision: beyond the face-to-face encounter. In J. Driscoll, *Practising clinical supervision: A reflective approach for healthcare professionals*, pp. 141–162. Bailliere Tindall.

Gibbs, G., 1988. *Learning by doing: A guide to teaching and learning methods.* Further Education Unit.

Jeffries, C. and Maeder, D.W., 2005. Using vignettes to build and assess teacher understanding of instructional strategies. *Professional Educator*, 27, pp. 17–28.

Kolb, D.A., 2014. *Experiential learning: Experience as the source of learning and development.* FT Press.

Lave, J. and Wenger, E., 1991. *Situated learning: Legitimate peripheral participation.* Cambridge University Press.

Moon, J.A., 2013. *A handbook of reflective and experiential learning: Theory and practice.* Routledge.

Naylor, S., 2020. Juggling the virtual balls as a programme leader. Available from https://www.advance-he.ac.uk/news-and-views/Juggling-the-virtual-balls-as-a-programme-leader (accessed 28 December 2021).

Schon, D.A., 2008. *The reflective practitioner: How professionals think in action.* Hachette UK.

1 Leadership

Applying leadership theory to programme leadership

You can enter programme leadership with no leadership training or qualifications and limited understanding of what the role entails (Gmelch and Buller, 2015). Leadership is a complex process with multiple dimensions which is extensively researched (Northouse, 2021). Although some are more popular than others there is no 'best' leadership style and different situations require different ones (Milliken, 1998). There are many different approaches to leadership, and although individuals may favour one approach, it is at times beneficial to draw on different approaches, particularly as the programme leader role holds low authoritative power over academic followers (Wolverton et al., 2005).

Transactional and transformational leadership

Transactional leadership has its limitations in the programme leader role because it relies on exchanges that occur between follower and leader often related to pay and working conditions (Northouse, 2021). Programme leaders manage the programme, but they do not have management responsibility for people. Therefore, it can feel like we have accountability for the programme but without any power (Murphy and Curtis, 2013). This means that the style of leadership adopted by the programme leader must consider this lack of authority. Programme leaders need to bring staff on board, often relying on persuasion and the goodwill of other people. From their interviews with programme leaders, Murphy and Curtis (2013) found that teaching duties were generally covered collegiately, and that somebody would step up to cover sessions, mark assignments, and so on. However, allocating workload, or making sure all the duties are covered, is a stressful aspect of the role.

We can see that one of the perceived barriers of being a leader is this lack of authority – no 'carrot or stick'. This means that you have no control over extrinsic motivation such as monetary rewards. Whilst these formal rewards may attract somebody to a job, they have less impact on their performance than intrinsic motivation, over which you have some control. I would argue

DOI: 10.4324/9781003126355-2

that rather than being a barrier this lack of authority can be an advantage. What do you think motivates your colleagues? Do you think they are motivated by money or how they feel about the job? Money will be a factor and people want to receive a fair wage, but it is usually the pride they take in their accomplishments that provides motivation. It is this that drives the quality of their work. People are driven by meaningful tasks that they perceive as valuable, things that are directly connected to them. Katzenbach and Khan (2010) talk about balancing formal and informal organisation. Formal organisation is about processes and procedures and rules. Informal organisation is concerned with generating emotional commitment. As programme leader, you are in a good position to foster informal organisation and steer it towards formal performance objectives. The key to this is identifying what makes people feel good about what they do and aligning this with the desired performance. How can you help foster pride in their work? How can you build intrinsic motivation?

Informal carrots can help to deliver what formal sticks cannot. As programme leader, you may not have any authority over an individual's formal performance review but you can create common goals for the programme delivery team as a means of motivation. These goals need to be meaningful, something they can take pride in achieving, but also taking pride in the journey to accomplishment. Metrics and analytics play a large part in higher education today and some of the goals are likely to be based on these. It is important not to fall back to these formal surveys and measurements and assume that people will be motivated by improving metrics scores. Goals for your programme should be derived from your team looking at what they personally want to achieve, for themselves, their module, and the programme. Confidence comes from achieving small goals and quite often small changes can make a big difference.

Transformational leadership has an emphasis on intrinsic motivation and the positive development of followers (Northouse, 2021). This fits with a work environment where followers want to be challenged and feel empowered but also have an inspirational leader to guide them (Bass et al., 1996). It has been suggested that the better leaders are more transformational than a leader who is passive and takes the laissez-faire approach that 'if it isn't broken then don't fix it' (Derue et al., 2011); or a leader who concentrates on corrective action if followers failed to comply (Bass et al., 1996; Derue et al., 2011). According to Levinson (1980), the 'carrot and stick' approach does not address the follower's sense of worth or gain their commitment and involvement. Central to transformational leadership is the ability to motivate others to do more than they originally intended or thought possible (Bass et al., 1996). Transformational leadership involves inspiring others to follow and commit to a shared vision or goal. Through mentoring, challenging, and supporting followers to be innovative problem solvers, followers develop their own leadership skills (Bass et al., 1996; Harms and Crede, 2010). More committed and satisfied followers are said to be produced by concentrating on clarifying the requirements of a task and then leaving the followers alone to complete the task unless there is a problem that needs support (Bass et al., 1996; Kirby et al.,

1992). Therefore, sometimes a laissez-faire approach is required to allow 'followers' to pursue their own solutions to issues thus affording them a degree of autonomy (Milliken, 1998; Blackmore et al., 2007). Transformational leaders act as mentors to their followers by encouraging learning achievement and personal development including leadership skills (Bass et al., 1996; Harms and Crede, 2010). As a programme leader, some of the academics in a follower role may be much more experienced than the programme leader thus the mentorship roles may be reversed with the follower acting as a mentor. However, the programme leader will also have student followers.

Collaborative and distributive leadership

Distributed leadership plays a role in higher education. There is more to this style than a delegation of tasks which can be seen with a top-down distribution of leadership. It is a leadership style that puts emphasis on collaboration rather than individual power and control where there is an ethos of shared responsibility, serving a common purpose. Distributed leadership broadens the basis for decision-making. It is appropriate in the programme leader context where leadership is distributed among the delivery team who work actively towards a common goal of delivering a programme. It is about using the skills and attributes of the team members and the division of labour of those working together, not about power over individuals. You can see how this can sit within a programme delivery team where the members with different skills and attributes work together to complete the common task of delivering the programme. Within programmes distributed leadership can take various forms depending on the make-up of the programme. Programmes with large numbers may have responsibility distributed to year tutors. Complex programmes may have various leads such as leads for placements, timetabling, assessments, and so on. For it to succeed there needs to be a climate of openness and trust with a platform for professional conversation and sharing practice. As programme leader, you need to let go of the responsibility and trust them to perform their role. You will need to encourage effective collaboration, support social interaction, and connect with others (Jones et al., 2012).

The benefits of a distributed approach include responsiveness, transparency, convenience, and teamwork (Bolden et al., 2008). Disadvantages include fragmentation, lack of role clarity, slow decision-making, and variations in individual capability (Bolden et al., 2008). Their research mainly looked at collective leadership from a senior management perspective, but they did recognise a source of leadership is from people without formal management roles as in the case of many programme leaders. Strong and inspiring leadership can give a sense of common purpose and direction and shape the values and cultures within the team. Thus, suggesting that collaborative and distributive leadership needs to work alongside other styles such a charismatic leadership. Messiah, hero, or the 'great man' leaders are solo figures who can exert charismatic power over a dependent passive workforce (Western, 2019). A passive workforce is not something you usually find in academia; therefore, a servant leadership approach should be considered.

Servant leadership

Servant leaders attempt to enhance the personal growth of their workforce and to improve the quality of care in the institution. This is achieved through team members' involvement in the decision-making and ethical caring behaviour (Spears, 1993). The overall idea of this is that the leader is to serve, focusing on the needs of others. This is an altruistic people-orientated approach, focusing less on processes and outcomes and more on the people involved. The principles of this type of leadership include listening, and paying attention to your team members. It is about displaying empathy, understanding their motivation, and having a good idea of their strengths and weaknesses. You are aiming to provide a healthy work environment and support a strong work–life balance, giving others the tools to succeed. Servant leaders have strong self-awareness and know the importance of self-reflection. They use persuasion to build consensus and share a vision. They lead by example and aim to build teams based on mutual trust and respect.

Servant leadership is not what it first appears, that you are a dog's body. You would soon burn out if you tried to sort out everyone's problems for them. As programme leader, your email in box would quickly get clogged up with questions and requests for help if this was the case. Servant leadership is about helping people to help themselves, facilitating meeting their needs, not taking responsibility for them (Wheeler, 2012). Investing the time and taking the approach of identifying what the person is aiming to achieve and how you can help will lead to greater self-sufficiency in the long term. An example of how this can work is when you get requests for information. Programme leaders hold a lot of information and are often the go-to person if someone, either student or colleague, wants to know something. Rather than answering the question or providing the information requested you instruct the person where to find the information for themselves. Empowering people in this way improves job satisfaction in the long term. Questionnaires undertaken in South Africa exploring the influence of servant leadership on job satisfaction found that servant leadership does improve job satisfaction, but acts of humility, self-sacrifice, and servanthood do not (Farrington and Lillah, 2019).

Servant leaders tend not to be showy or pretentious; they are modest, not taking individual credit for achievements (Van Dierendonck, 2011). If you are driven by the need for self-acclaim or are motivated by being in the spotlight, servant leadership may not be the best approach for you. However, it is an approach that you can use to get the best from your team when there is no direct managerial authority, such as programme leadership. Literature suggests servant leadership is effective in service-orientated organisations such as higher education (Farrington and Lillah, 2019).

This type of leadership should produce a highly motivated team in which morale is high. Motivation and morale are also improved due to collaborative decision-making. Looking over the principles you can see this is a very ethical form of leadership. It is not without its disadvantages. Relationship building takes time and members need to engage with the process. It therefore will not work in every situation and there will be times when a more dictatorial approach will be required. With collaborative decision-making, a consensus may not always be reached amicably, and you may have to strike a balance between collaboration against meeting fixed goals from the institution. Time is often a factor and sometimes decisions need to be made so quickly that it does not allow time for collaboration. It is sometimes easier for you as a programme leader to make decisions without wider consultation. This goes against the whole ethos of a servant leader. Personal ego does not fit within servant leadership; this can be an issue in an organisation where there is performance-related pay or rewards. However, if you focus primarily on the growth and well-being of your academic delivery team it will inevitably have a knock-on effect on the development and well-being of your students.

Eco-leadership

It is clear that the style of leadership can have an impact on the quality of student learning (Martin et al., 2003). However, it is not just about the academic staff and students. In today's higher education there is a greater importance placed on the requirement of other stakeholders such as placement providers (Martin et al., 2003). Western (2019) suggests a leadership discourse, which he terms eco-leadership. He uses the term ecology, the study of the interrelations of the living specimens and the environment, and human ecology, the study of humans and their relationships to the environment (Western, 2019). This theory is about connectivity in a complex uncertain environment. It is less concerned with leading change and more about creating an environment where there is the capacity to handle ambivalence and uncertainty. In the current climate of uncertainty and rapid change within higher education, there is definitely an advantage to drawing on this theory.

Eco-leadership conceptualises ecosystems within ecosystems. It recognises that organisations are interdependent and that areas within organisations are interlinked. Change in one area impacts on another. Think about when a change is made to one module, such as changing the date of an assessment, and how this might impact on other modules. Eco leadership seeks to break down the protectionist silo approach, utilising communities of practice and distributive leadership to enable collaborative, collective wisdom. Today's world sees an explosion in the capacity for networking. This is vital to the success of an organisation required to adapt to financial, political, and global changes. There is a moral and ethical element to eco leadership. This goes beyond personal and organisation values, looking to wider ethical implications.

Areas that are prominent in higher education include social mobilisation and Black, Asian, and Minority Ethnic inequalities.

In the current environment the interdependence with stakeholders, customers, and regulators has never been so apparent. Eco-leadership enables an organisation to react to a fast-changing environment. The symbiotic relationship with the social, technological, political, natural, and economic environments can result in huge challenges. Eco-leadership is an emerging theory that helps us face these challenges. It is an ethical leadership approach aligning the challenges of organisational success, social responsibility, and environmental sustainability, eco-leadership sees these challenges as not competing but integral to each other.

As with servant leadership, eco-leadership has a focus on people rather than material gain, putting importance on communities and friendship. It recognises the importance of organisational belonging. This is developed through mutuality, solidarity, and engagement. Eco-leadership is a form of distributive leadership. It is a practical and robust approach to leadership, creating feedback from the edges to inform the centre; that is, creating a mechanism of feedback from both staff, students, stakeholders, and so on.

We can think of organisations as ecosystems with webs of connecting networks. Smaller ecosystems interconnect and are interdependent with other ecosystems producing a larger ecosystem. From a programme leader's perspective each module can be viewed as an ecosystem. These are connected to form the whole programme. The programme will form its own ecosystem and will connect beyond its boundaries. For example, student support, professional services, a placement team will all be in their own ecosystem interconnecting and interdependent with each programme. Connections and networks between each ecosystem are vital to success. If the module leader makes a change to their module in isolation rather than seeing the bigger picture of the whole programme it could impact on the student experience.

One of the main qualities of eco-leadership is connectivity: recognising our interdependence with each other and the environment. As a programme leader, you need to explore whom you need to make connections with. Keeping with the metaphor of ecology, these connections will continually be changing, forming, and re-forming. It is valuable to keep a list of the connections you have made. Have this as a live document with names and contact numbers and organisations or departments. You will find it invaluable to connect to other programme leaders. Universities often facilitate this via activities such as programme leader forums. If not, you may find it useful to connect to other programme leaders via your own networks. As a programme leader one of your roles will be to facilitate connectivity between the teaching staff on the programme. This can be via regular team meetings, electronic chat platforms, or other methods. This will be discussed further later in the chapter. You also need to connect regularly and effectively with students.

Ways of doing this are discussed in Chapter 3 on quality and Chapter 4 on programme design and approval.

Trait theory of leadership

The lack of managerial authority of programme leaders suggests that an element of trait theory of leadership is necessary. Trait theory assumes that leadership depends on personal qualities (Northouse, 2021). This theory dates from the early 1900s and fell out of favour due to the lack of backing from research (Judge et al., 2002). There are few if any universal traits associated with effective leadership. However, there are some common traits such as self-confidence, emotional intelligence, conscientiousness, and integrity (Judge et al., 2002). Leader behaviours have a greater impact on effective leadership than leader traits. It is behaviour, rather than personality, that will inspire followers. Effective academic leadership is supported by the behaviours of building communities, setting direction, and empowering others, which is

Table 1.1 Leadership theories

Leadership theory	*Main concept*	*Application to programme leadership*
Transactional leadership	Reward and punishment	Access and become familiar with the metrics and analytics which are prominent in HE today.
Transformational leadership	Identify change and create a vision	Motivate others to change through mentoring and support. This is applicable for both staff and students.
Collaborative leadership	Interdependence and shared responsibility	Encourage collaboration between individuals delivering the programme.
Distributed leadership	Leadership is distributed throughout the organisation	Distribute aspects of programme leadership, for example with year tutors.
Servant leadership *Robert Greenleaf*	A caring style of leadership helping people to develop	Focus on the needs of others and help them to help themselves.
Eco-leadership *Simon Western*	Recognising the need for networking and interdependence	Make connections with other people and departments which impact on the programme delivery.
Trait theory of leadership	Based on the characteristics or personal qualities of a person	Certain traits promote effective leadership. Become aware of these to enable you to develop them.

more achievable than characteristics such as being intelligent, intuitive, and self-assured (Rowley, 1997). Behaviour can be considered and adapted; it is therefore logical to conclude that leadership skills can be learned and developed rather than being born a leader (Derue et al., 2011). In the past little attention has been paid to the development of programme leaders (Wolverton et al., 2005; Blackmore et al., 2007). Due to this lack of training and mentorship encountered by many programme leaders, learning from experience rather than training has been the way they have developed leadership skills. Interpersonal skills are of great importance in programme leadership. In the next section leadership skills of motivating, networking, building collegiality, and dealing with difficult people are explored.

Table 1.1 provides an overview of some leadership theories and how they apply to programme leaders.

Skills for programme leadership

Motivating

Pride is a very strong motivational driver. Inherently people need to feel good about what they do and how they do it. This needs to go beyond the outcome, ultimately the student success, and be broken down into small everyday tasks. How do you motivate academics through stressful busy times? One thing that can make a difference is having personal informal connections and knowing what works for different individuals. This requires strong interpersonal skills such as active listening, showing empathy, flexibility, and patience. Generally, pride needs an audience, as individuals want to share good feelings. This has become quite prominent in today's social media. The audience may be family and friends, but equally it could be the person's day-to-day work colleagues. Reactions of the audience impact on the feelings of pride. As programme leader, you can encourage those feelings of pride by recognising accomplishments on a personal level. Rather than sending out blanket emails – for example, 'Well done team' – think about sending carefully crafted personalised emails or notes. You could copy in the person's line manager to extend the audience and thus impact. Become a master motivator by being observant, learning how to make people feel good about the work they must do. As a leader aim to motivate people intrinsically and help them achieve their personal best.

There are times in the academic calendar when it is challenging to motivate people. Academics may be busy marking trying to get through assessment workload at the same time as you are trying to encourage them to plan ready for the following year. So how do you keep people energised, working to their individual best? How do you get them focused on a vision when they are bogged down in the mundane? One way is to tune into the potential of each person by appreciating them and making them feel good about the contribution they are making. Respect is an important aspect of motivation; it is therefore important to give respect as well as expecting to receive it. To get the best out of people you need to maintain positive relationships despite different personality styles or working preferences. Reach out to people who may be challenging. People cope in different ways. Some academics during a marking period may bury themselves in the work in order to plough through it. This may work for them, but as programme leader you may require them to engage with other programme-related tasks at the same time. This requires mutual respect. Respect the way they prefer to work, but also instil in them respect and understanding of the requirements of the wider programme. As programme leader, you do need to obtain a degree of control. However, distributing power to others to make decisions will help increase pride in their abilities. It will give them more ownership over their module and contribution to the programme, and possibly pride in the fact that they have been trusted with the responsibility.

Networking

Networking is an accepted part of academic life. There are benefits of networking in helping develop a strong professional identity and advance your career. Today it is considered an essential professional activity, as social networking can raise your profile and that of your programme, particularly if you have an online presence that can be 'searchable', giving you increased visibility. Networking within your organisation is equally important and this is discussed further in Chapter 2.

In today's digital environment social media is a valuable tool for networking. Online tools can be used to find and keep in touch with academics with similar interests. They can help you discover new people and keep you in touch with former colleagues who have knowledge and experience from which you can benefit. A wide network even if the ties are quite weak can be valuable for sharing information, gaining inspiration, and a form of mentoring. As well as people, social networking platforms help you keep up to date with current issues with the benefit of being able to see a variety of people's views on any issues. Novice programme leaders can struggle with political aspects of leadership (Murphy and Curtis, 2013). From a programme leaders' point of view, it can be a real advantage if you can be up to date with challenges in higher education and see how people are approaching and addressing these challenges. Professional and government bodies regularly use platforms such as Twitter as a form of communication and to disseminate information. Another recent development is the surge in 'tweeting' from conferences which are revolutionising professional networking and information sharing (Power, 2015).

Jordan and Weller (2018) explored the benefits, problems, and tensions in professional engagement with online networking using a secondary analysis of a survey. They report that social media platforms can be very powerful tools for relationship building, removing any geographical boundaries. There is clear value in providing a platform for the dissemination of research and for identifying and building research collaborations. Concerns about the time involved in engaging with social networks was a principal problem identified. Not only do you need time to actively engage with the network, you also get spam emails related to each social network platform. There are currently many platforms and it would be very time-consuming to engage with too many of them. It is worth spending some time exploring which will be most valuable to you.

Another barrier identified was about digital literacy, recognising that some people do not particularly enjoy or feel comfortable networking using these platforms (Jordan and Weller, 2018). Not all academics perceive social media platforms as being useful or have concerns about the reliability of information posted. The more you engage in these the more you are motivated to use them, and the more proficient you become (Donelan, 2016). Concern has been raised about commercialisation, that as an academic you may be linked to marketing and adverts promoted on the sites (Jordan and Weller, 2018). One point raised was about mixing personal and professional life (Jordan and Weller, 2018). Although social media platforms support multiple profiles, using more than one may add an unnecessary level of complexity, considering that personal and professional values should be aligned. It is important to manage your online persona and it goes without saying that you should not be a keyboard warrior but act as professionally online as you would in person (Power, 2015). As engagement with social media is an expectation of an academic, you could try scheduling social media time into your weekly diary. Taking a strategic approach to social media will help you use networking platforms to your advantage rather than it being unwanted added pressure on your workload.

Many self-help guides and courses are available in how to develop your networking skills. Here are some useful tips:

- View networking as a learning opportunity rather than a chore, a chance to discover something new. You never know what may come out of a brief conversation, sparking new ideas.
- Avoid a scatter-gun approach, know who will be at an event or whom you will potentially networking with. Do your homework, find out about these people, what their research and other interests are. If possible, find a common interest.
- Take the approach of 'giver's gain'. Think about what you can give to others, a unique perspective or information, something that you can share.
- Set goals; if you know, for example, that you're going to a particular conference, rather than randomly walking around the exhibition, have an aim of connecting with two or three specific people.
- To initiate or join a conversation start the transaction by asking a question; this is often easier than giving your opinion. Introverts are often very good listeners; this is a great advantage in networking as a person who has an attentive audience will remember the conversation. Networking isn't about being the centre of attention or vivacious, it is about creating long-term relationships and contacts.

Building collegiality

Looking at the theories of leadership in relation to the programme leader, you want a highly motivated team that works well together in a collaborative way. To do this you need to develop an environment of openness and trustworthiness, one in which there is effective connectivity. Here are some practical suggestions:

Your team is a collection of individuals with their own strengths and weaknesses. You can start by identifying and recognising these. People are not always good at recognising their own attributes and it would be useful if there was a way of supporting this. This could be via a mentoring system or peer review. You could facilitate an open discussion as part of a team meeting about people's strengths and weaknesses. Open discussion is an effective way of understanding individual talents which can lead to the formation of mutually beneficial connections.

Setting goals is important for providing a focus on what needs achieving. There is likely to be some direction for these; for example, an action plan acting on feedback from the National Student Survey. Build a sense of ownership within the team by mutually setting the goals rather than imposing them. When it comes to delivering on those actions you can demonstrate trust in your team by establishing what needs to be done but not dictating how it should be done. It is important to have mutual respect and understand that team members may not do things in the way that you would.

Leaders are often role models and showing that you are reliable and dependable – for example, by responding to communications in a timely manner and undertaking tasks that you have promised to do – will build your team's trust in you.

It is important that you know your team members and that your team know each other. Meeting with your team on a regular basis will help to develop closer relationships. Building and nurturing relationships can also be facilitated in less formal ways such as social activities and connecting via social media. Take time to get to know your colleagues on a personal level. Recognise and celebrate both team and individual successes as this will increase motivation. Cliques and personality clashes may occur; it is only by addressing these that they can be discouraged.

Dealing with difficult people

Programme leaders are not the only ones to have to deal with difficult people. However, with the responsibility of running a programme and student satisfaction potentially at stake it is important that the outcome of any dealings with people is as positive as possible. What each of us perceive as a difficult person will vary. Lilley (2019, p. 8) states: 'There is no such thing as a difficult person. There are just people we need to learn how to deal with.' There are people who appear to relish the opportunity to be provocative and fuel an argument. Some people are protectionist, who put a barrier up around themselves and may not engage with the requirements of the programme as you would like them to do. There are people who appear to always be busy, with no time to fulfil tasks that are required of the programme. Programme leaders interact with many people – academics, students, administrators, and placement links. At some point you will encounter someone whom you perceive as being difficult; this section provides some tips on how to get the best out of these interactions, focusing on what can be controlled, which is our reactions.

If someone is being difficult it is tempting to be difficult back, reflecting their behaviour. Doing this will not get positive results. Stay calm and in control, demonstrating the professional behaviour you expect from others. Listening is a large part of communication. Acknowledge what the other person is saying, try to understand their actions, or point of view. It is important to actively listen, reflecting back what they are saying, or how they are acting; for example, 'I can see you are angry'. By listening you can try to work out what is making them act in the manner you perceive as negative.

Consider what else might be going on in their life that is making them difficult. It is rare to have nothing impacting on one's behaviour. It is an interesting thought that if everyone in a room put their problems in a basket, you would most likely want to take your own back again rather than someone else's. Therefore, don't be too quick to judge; if someone is being difficult it might be driven by vulnerability or stress, not belligerence or aggression. Emotional intelligence is an important quality in a leader and this is discussed more in Chapter 3. Having the capacity to be aware of others' emotions, recognising when acting with kindness and compassion is required, is a valuable skill. It is also helpful to find some common ground; a personal connection helps to generate a smoother conversation. Get to know the person behind the actions. Treat them with respect; belittling their ideas or actions will only build bigger barriers to a positive outcome, not help to resolve a situation.

As with any conflict, staying calm is essential. It is easy to become angry; when we find someone or something infuriating, this is not the right time to deal with an issue. Having the ability to remain patient and calm will help de-escalate a situation. You need to try and clearly articulate your views; providing context around your opinions will help the difficult person have a better understanding of the issue. People are less resistant to you if they have background information to enable them to empathise with your situation, or what you are trying to achieve.

Shine the spotlight inwards, examine your actions. Someone else may consider you to be that difficult person. Is there something that you are doing that is making the situation more difficult than it needs to be? Are you being as open and receptive to others as you could be? More importantly, are you perceived as being open to the opinion of others?

There are some things that you may not have control over; focus on those things that you can control. It might be that someone is not doing what you ask them to; you could keep persevering with them, or you might find better results looking for someone else to help with the situation. Do not dwell on the past, or bring up previous situations; focus on moving forward to find a solution. It can be useful to seek advice from others. You may have colleagues, managers, or others who have experienced a similar situation. They may be able to help you view things from a different angle or offer a solution. Some situations may need escalating to a higher authority.

It is tempting to either put off dealing with a situation or put up with it. As a programme leader, you cannot always avoid confrontation. A fear of engaging in conflict when it is required can lead to losing control, or the loss of respect for both you as programme leader and the programme Remember, conflict is not always a negative thing; it can be the path to resolution. Try not to get defensive, or take things too personally; even though what someone says in the heat of the moment may come across as personal, it is more likely that the difficult person is more upset about a situation than you.

Vignette

I can identify with the allocation of teaching being stressful. One of the programmes I have led had weekly tutorials and practical sessions that were related to the programme as a whole rather than allocated to a particular module. This meant that the module leaders did not have ownership of these sessions and they needed to be allocated to teaching staff from across the whole programme. At the time there were some personality clashes within the delivery team and on frequent occasions this resulted in some heated staff meetings. My aim was to allocate the sessions in an open transparent way so that each person had a choice in the sessions they took and that the workload was spread fairly across the team. I arranged a programme planning meeting and as part of that meeting included the allocation of the teaching sessions. At this point, the timetable had been produced so everyone was aware when the sessions were to be delivered. This meant that people would have an idea if they were available to take sessions. I went to the meeting prepared with each session printed on a different piece of card including information about the topic and the date of delivery. The cards were colour coded according to the year group. At the allocated time in the meeting, I produced the cards and spread them over a large table. I knew how many sessions there were and gave the staff an idea of how many sessions they should be picking up. In the first phase, staff moved around the table and took the cards relating to sessions they wanted to teach. There was time for them to check these against their diary and ensure there were no clashes in the sessions they took and that they had an even workload across the year. After a period of time the staff took a seat around the table and arranged their cards in front of them. Putting them into year groups and lining up according to the date they could clearly see the spread of their workload. The workload of each person was transparent to everyone. Inevitably there were some sessions remaining in the centre of the table unclaimed. This required a period of negotiation. Staff members with a low number of cards needed to pick up more sessions from the pack. However, if the remaining topics were not within their area of expertise there was time for negotiation with other staff and sessions were swopped. This exercise resulted in all the sessions having a named academic. People were happy with most of the sessions as they had picked them. Inevitably they were less happy with some of the sessions but as these were in the minority it was more acceptable that just being given teaching sessions they did not want. They had some control over the situation which reduces stress.

This particular teaching workload was allocated for the whole year, so it all sounds great. However, it was not all smoothly delivered from a programme leader's point of view. Although I had stressed that the sessions were now the responsibility of the person they had been allocated to I did get periodic emails from one or two staff saying, 'I have a meeting to go to and can no longer cover this session'. It felt quite a tough thing to do but my response was that the session was their responsibility to find cover. They could negotiate a swop with a colleague or find an alternative person from a pool of associate lecturers. As programme leader, I did feel responsible for the student experience and if someone did not turn up to take a session it would be problematic. This caused some anxiety. I sent out meeting requests to the staff members covering the sessions. Most accepted but it was awkward when one declined a couple of their sessions. I needed to approach them and ask why. Thankfully it was just a mistake, the click of a wrong button. Initially – until my confidence in the system increased – I would check my colleagues' diaries to ensure the sessions were in their calendar which gave me reassurance. There is no control over staff sickness and if this happened at short notice with no one available to step in students were given some self-directed study. Longer-term staff absence sessions were covered through goodwill. Staff members are more likely to do this if there is a collegiate environment.

On reflection, this method of allocating sessions worked. I had no managerial authority to make people cover the teaching. This method was open and transparent. There was an element of peer pressure as those with a smaller workload in front of them could clearly see this. One member of staff did try to explain their lack of sessions due to other commitments in the 'pipeline' but the teaching was given suitable recognition in staff workload. There was a slight worry that if a person reluctantly took a session that was not really wanted, they would find a way of not covering it, but this did not happen and realistically I had confidence in my colleague's academic professionalism. Overall, staff had sessions that they wanted to teach which has a positive impact on staff satisfaction and a knock-on effect on student satisfaction.

Reflection

Programme leaders are usually the first port of call if students have not had a response from another member of staff, for example a personal tutor or module leader. Using the knowledge about styles of leadership contained in this chapter, critically reflect on this thinking about the implications and how you could deal with this situation.

- Why might the student have contacted the programme leader?
- Why might the student feel that has not had a response?
- What impact might this situation have on a programme leader?
- What immediate actions could you as programme leader take?
- What long-term actions could you take?

Considerations

From the student perspective they may have unrealistic expectations, and in these days of instant messaging expect an instant response, thus contact the programme leader after no response was received within a few minutes. However, the student may be having a crisis and need an instant response. They may have had past experience of getting a poor response from a particular person, so they quickly look for another respondent. Alternatively, they may have waited a few days and not received a response.

From the academic perspective, they may have been off sick, on leave, turned off email notifications to concentrate on another task such as marking. They may have hundreds of emails and missed the one from this student. They may have 'responding to the student' on their to-do list.

From the programme-leader perspective, emails like this just add to their workload. They may find it irritating and feel like they are picking up work from other people. They may view the student as overly demanding. It may be a recurring problem with one member of staff.

Implications of this incident could be poor student experience leading to poor student reviews. The student could have an issue that if not addressed could lead to a bigger problem and more work.

Immediate action required is that the student needs a response, but if you sort out the issue it does not provide a long-term solution. You could check the availability for the staff member, i.e. that they are not off work, then email the student copying in the member of staff. This results in the student receiving an acknowledgement of their issue and the member of staff is aware that the student has contacted you. This is an open and transparent approach. The member of staff is made aware of the student's issue and that it needs dealing with. After all, they, not you as programme leader, are likely to be the most appropriate person to deal with it. If the member of staff is not going to be available within a reasonable timeframe you may need to deal with the situation, or if it can wait let the student know the expected timeframe for a response.

Long-term actions that may prevent this from happening include managing student expectations by having an email response policy. The member of staff may benefit from 'managing their in-box' training. A flow chart for students detailing whom to contact in an emergency may divert email traffic away from you. Promoting consistent use of the 'out of office' facility for email makes students aware of the staff member's availability and expected response time. An open discussion at a team meeting will raise awareness of the problem and allow team members to offer solutions.

Summary

This first chapter covers the topic of leadership which is an essential part of being a programme leader. Different leadership theories have been discussed including transactional, transformational, collaborative, distributive, servant, eco, and trait. The chapter covered an overview of each theory and how they might apply to the role of programme leader. There are essential skills required of a programme leader including motivating, networking, building collegiality, and dealing with difficult people. A rationale has been included for each of these skills followed by practical advice that you may find useful in developing your role. The vignette tells about the experience of one programme leader trying to allocate teaching sessions to academic staff and how they approached this. Questions are used to guide you in reflecting on how you would deal with a situation typically experienced by programme leaders.

References

Bass, B.M., Avolio, B.J., and Atwater, L., 1996. The transformational and transactional leadership of men and women. *Applied Psychology*, 45(1), pp. 5–34.

Blackmore, P., Dales, R., Law, S., and Yates, P., 2007. Investigating the capabilities of course and module leaders in departments. Higher Education Academy, York. Available at www.academia.edu/download/44877342/Investigating_the_capabilities_of_course20160418–20163342-in1ap4.pdf (28 November 2021).

Bolden, R., Petrov, G., and Gosling, J., 2008. *Developing collective leadership in higher education*. Leadership Foundation for Higher Education.

Derue, D.S., Nahrgang, J.D., Wellman, N.E.D., and Humphrey, S.E., 2011. Trait and behavioral theories of leadership: An integration and meta-analytic test of their relative validity. *Personnel Psychology*, 64(1), pp. 7–52.

Donelan, H., 2016. Social media for professional development and networking opportunities in academia. *Journal of Further and Higher Education*, 40(5), pp. 706–729.

Farrington, S.M. and Lillah, R., 2019. Servant leadership and job satisfaction within private healthcare practices. *Leadership in Health Services*, 32(1), pp. 148–168.

Gmelch, W.H. and Buller, J.L., 2015. *Building academic leadership capacity: A guide to best practices*. John Wiley & Sons.

Harms, P.D. and Credé, M., 2010. Emotional intelligence and transformational and transactional leadership: A meta-analysis. *Journal of Leadership & Organizational Studies*, 17(1), pp. 5–17.

Jones, S., Lefoe, G., Harvey, M., and Ryland, K., 2012. Distributed leadership: A collaborative framework for academics, executives and professionals in higher education. *Journal of Higher Education Policy and Management*, 34(1), pp. 67–78.

Jordan, K. and Weller, M., 2018. Academics and social networking sites: Benefits, problems and tensions in professional engagement with online networking. *Journal of Interactive Media in Education*, 2018(1). doi:10.5334/jime.448.

Judge, T.A., Bono, J.E., Ilies, R., and Gerhardt, M.W., 2002. Personality and leadership: a qualitative and quantitative review. *Journal of Applied Psychology*, 87(4), pp. 765–780.

Katzenbach, J.R. and Khan, Z., 2010. *Leading outside the lines: How to mobilize the informal organization, energize your team, and get better results*. John Wiley & Sons.

Kirby, P.C., Paradise, L.V., and King, M.I., 1992. Extraordinary leaders in education: Understanding transformational leadership. *The Journal of Educational Research*, 85(5), pp. 303–311.

Levinson, H., 1980. Power, leadership, and the management of stress. *Professional Psychology*, 11(3), pp. 497–508.

Lilley, R., 2019. *Dealing with difficult people: fast, effective strategies for handling problem people*. 4th edition. Kogan Page.

Martin, E., Trigwell, K., Prosser, M., and Ramsden, P., 2003. Variation in the experience of leadership of teaching in higher education. *Studies in Higher Education*, 28(3), pp. 247–259.

Milliken, J., 1998. The cult of academic leadership. *Higher Education in Europe*, 23(4), pp. 505–515.

Murphy, M. and Curtis, W., 2013. The micro-politics of micro-leadership: Exploring the role of programme leader in English universities. *Journal of Higher Education Policy and Management*, 35(1), pp. 34–44.

Northouse, P.G., 2021. *Leadership: Theory and practice*. Sage.

Power, A., 2015. Twitter's potential to enhance professional networking. *British Journal of Midwifery*, 23(1), pp. 65–67.

Rowley, J., 1997. Academic leaders: Made or born? *Industrial and Commercial Training*, 29(3), pp. 78–84.

Spears, L., 1993. Trustees as servant-leaders: A report and reference guide. *International Journal of Value-Based Management*, 6(1), pp. 83–99.

Van Dierendonck, D., 2011. *Servant leadership: A review and synthesis. Journal of Management*, 37(4), pp. 1228–1261.

Western, S., 2019. *Leadership: A critical text*. Sage.

Wheeler, D.W., 2012. *Servant leadership for higher education: Principles and practices.* John Wiley & Sons.

Wolverton, M., Ackerman, R., and Holt, S., 2005. Preparing for leadership: What academic department chairs need to know. *Journal of Higher Education Policy and Management*, 27(2), pp. 227–238.

2 Your support mechanisms

Support is available if you know where to look

If you search 'programme leader support' the main thing you get from various universities is information about the roles and responsibilities of programme leadership, of which there are many. Some universities provide a programme leader handbook, specifically marketing these as offering guidance to new programme leaders. These can be useful documents, but they tend to provide more detail about the responsibilities, focusing on what the programme leader needs to do. Useful information is provided such as main contacts and links to further documents such as assessment regulations. These handbooks can quickly go out of date and would need updating at least annually, but as policy and procedure within universities rapidly change it is likely that something will have changed as soon as a handbook is published.

Various programme leader courses exist, some within institutions and others from external organisations. These generally cover curriculum design, learning and teaching approaches, organisation of a programme, and pedagogy. In essence covering different aspects of what is required for leading a programme. Advance HE (2021) recognises the importance of the role of programme leader. They provide a programme aimed at supporting and enhancing programme leadership. This is a positive step forward, but engagement with this may be inhibited by cost or the timing of the programme. Looking at the modules offered, this programme supported the programme leader in aspects such as leadership, exploring the context of higher education, teaching and learning, and student experience, essentially supporting the development of the programme leader in their role. The Staff and Education Development Association (SEDA) (2021), a professional association for staff and educational developers in the UK, has a similar approach in that much of the content contains information for supporting the role.

There is recognition within some universities of the need for leadership skills amongst their staff members. This manifests as leadership programmes using a variety of approaches including workshops, online resources, mentoring, and reflection. Although there are transferable skills, these tend to be

DOI: 10.4324/9781003126355-3

focused more on aspiring managers than programme leaders. Some institutions provide well-thought-out programmes which recognise the challenges programme leaders face, that it can be a lonely role and thus facilitate meeting other programme leaders. Some leadership programmes also support the development of an application for fellow or senior fellow of the Advance HE.

This chapter starts by looking at supporting the individual behind the programme leader role; that is, support available to you as a person so you are better equipped holistically to fulfil your role. Because being aware of a problem you can start to address the issues, later the chapter explores different forms of stressors and how to reduce their impact.

Peer support

Peer support can be an invaluable mechanism that will help you fulfil your role as programme leader. It not only offers a sense of belonging, helping you identify with your role, it also provides a platform for feedback. It is well established for use in behaviour change, often in the form of self-help groups, for example for alcoholism or slimming. It is also used in the development of new skills and for coping with medical or mental health issues. Siegel (2000) suggested that peer relationships could be used as an alternative to mentoring for personal and professional growth. Your peers, other new programme leaders, are likely to identify with your situation than more than established staff (Parker et al., 2008).

There is value in sharing experiences with other programme leaders, as long as this is in a non-threatening environment (Cahill et al., 2015). It will help you develop a sense of identity in your new role as programme leader and reduce feelings of isolation. Some institutions offer peer support in the form of programme leader forums (Ellis and Nimmo, 2018). These tend to focus on the day-to-day requirements of the role, which can be very useful information (Cahill et al., 2015). Literature on peer support for new programme leaders is sparse. However, it has been recognised as having a role for those new to teaching at university (Turner et al., 2016). It has value for workers early in their career and may have a significant impact on the retention of programme leaders (Chenot et al., 2009). It can also support career development (Parker et al., 2008). Peer support links to social learning theory in that individuals can learn from a credible role model and from interaction with peers who are coping well in a situation (Solomon, 2004). Thus peer support can be valuable if you find yourself struggling with any aspect of the role.

You may find that moral support from colleagues can help you build self-confidence and promote situated learning within your role. Eraut (2000) suggested a triangular relationship between challenge, support, and confidence as factors that affect learning in the workplace. For novice professionals to progress, they need to be challenged without being so daunted that it reduces their confidence (Eraut, 2007). Thus, a step-by-step approach to learning and development should smooth the transition of new programme leaders.

Vygotsky, a Russian psychologist (well known to early years educators), has theories that can be adapted to the learning and development of adults. His emphasis was on social interaction in learning and he is known for his concept of the zone of proximal development, which explores the relationship between learning and development (Vygotsky and Cole, 1978).

The zone of proximal development is the gap between what someone can do unaided and what they might be able to do with support (Daniels, 2005; Smidt, 2009). This support may come in the form of an expert who helps the novice to take the steps to move from dependence to independence (Daniels, 2005; Smidt, 2009). Learners were more likely to reach their potential when they were supported by those with whom they shared cultural tools, for example a common language (Bruner, 1996; Smidt, 2009). Scaffolding, as a form of structured support, was introduced by psychologist Jerome Bruner (Fleer 1990). With scaffolding, support is gradually removed, as mastery of the task is achieved (Bruner et al., 1956; Smidt, 2009). Vygotsky suggested that a person can only imitate that which is within their development level (Vygotsky and Cole, 1978). Thus, learning and removal of support should be matched with the individual's development level (Vygotsky and Cole, 1978). This indicates that a more formal process of mentoring could be a valuable source of support for a programme leader.

Mentoring

Mentoring is essentially a one-to-one relationship with a more experienced person who can act as an advisor, coach, role model, and so on. Your institution may have a mentoring scheme in place and offer you a mentor specifically for your role as programme leader, or you may create your own informal mentoring relationship. Either way, it is helpful to understand mentorship in order to gain the most from it. It is a recognised development tool that can help you acclimatise to the role (Knippelmeyeer and Torraco, 2007; Carmel and Paul, 2015).

There is confusion about the term mentor, as what people call mentoring sometimes appears to be more like supervision. This can be effective at helping manage work-related problems (Bell et al., 2017). Having a mentor as a named 'go-to' person for advice can be useful but it is likely to be the case that a new programme leader will not know what they need to know. Morton-Cooper and Palmer (1999) stated the need for clarification so that people can plan and prepare for the relationship. It is therefore valuable to have structure to the relationship with mentees and their mentors being clear about the purpose of the mentorship, otherwise this relationship is inhibited in its use as a support mechanism. This scenario was seen in the research undertaken by Eraut (2007) where all their participants were provided a dedicated mentor but most support was provided by 'helpful others'. According to Boud and Middleton (2003), only a few of the people whom individuals learn from at work are recognised by organisations as someone having a role in promoting learning such as a mentor. A scheme in which regular meetings are pre-arranged throughout the year could pre-empt key stress points for a programme leader.

What makes a good mentoring scheme?

A plethora of literature is available on mentoring. Below are some ideas on how to get the most out of a mentoring relationship:

- You need to build a relationship. There needs to be trust between mentor and mentee so that you feel comfortable discussing your experiences and issues. Looking at mentoring for new lecturers, Turner et al. (2016) highlighted the importance of the choice of mentor with factors such as proximity, experience, and knowledge impacting on the success of the relationship.
- Good communication. This is a two-way process; there will be little value for you if when you want to talk about something and raise a topic, your mentor spends the rest of the session talking about their experiences. Mentors primarily need to listen. It may be useful to pre-determine the topics you wish to discuss.
- You want your mentee to probe and challenge. This way they can help you focus on the main issue and help you develop your own solutions. There should be a focus on constructive feedback.
- Your mentor should be someone who can draw on their own experience in order to offer a different perspective. A mentee should be open to looking at an issue through different lenses.
- Mentoring should have a structure to any meetings which include an element of reflection and action planning.
- Mentoring as a process. A mentoring relationship should have a beginning, a middle, and importantly an end, bringing the relationship to a formal close. The arrangement can be short or long term depending on the requirement of the scheme. Formal mentoring schemes for new academics tend to be for a year (Carmel and Paul, 2015). This is a logical timescale for a programme leader due to the annual cycle of programmes.
- Your mentor can be a useful source for increasing your network. From their experience, they will know whom the best people to approach about particular issues. They can signpost to further support.

Networking

Networking was discussed in Chapter 1 regarding leadership. This mainly focused on external networks. Internal networks can be very supportive for a programme leader. Programme leader forums do help foster relationships with peers. They often have ‘guests’ such as representatives from quality or a learning enhancement team who come to talk about current issues. This is useful for putting faces to names and for building your list of contacts. Networking within the organisation is a way of sharing knowledge, promoting discussion, sharing practice, and problem-solving. As well as meeting with other programme leaders' communities of practices or hubs may be in existence that you could use to increase your network. These could be research hubs or special interest groups in specific areas of academic practice. Any platform where you meet new people, either virtually or face to face, can provide a mechanism of support. You are effectively building a community of people who could help or advise you in a particular aspect of your role. Conversations could spark new ideas, increase your understanding of the workings of the institution, create new opportunities in terms of career development, to name but a few reasons to network.

Communities of practice

Programme leader forums can be a valuable source of support when starting in the role as programme leader when may be inundated with a plethora of new terminology and processes. Communities of practice can be a useful way to view an individual's interaction with a group such as a programme leader forum. According to anthropologists Lave and Wenger (1991), communities of practice are a group of people who share an interest or profession. They can occur anywhere, often so familiar that they are overlooked. However, when they are given a name and brought into focus this concept becomes a perspective that can help in understanding our world better. Their concept, built on work with apprenticeships, is that of situated learning and legitimate peripheral participation in a community of practice. This suggested that as newcomers join an established group, they start on the periphery watching and learning how the group works and how they can participate. Programme leaders do not often have the luxury of this as they are usually thrown into this pivotal role.

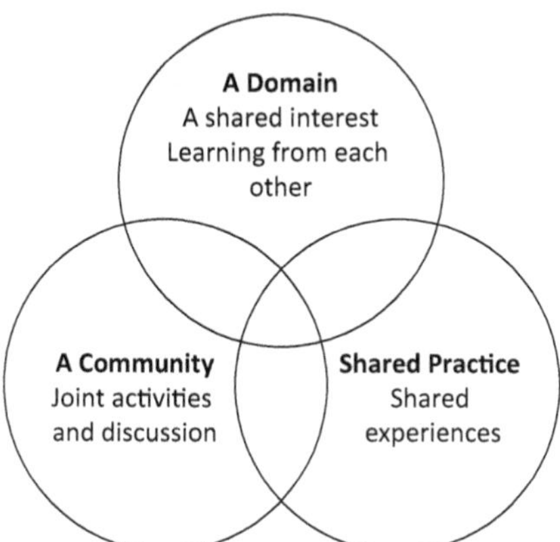

Figure 2.1 Elements of a community of practice

The community of practice exists through the combination of three elements, a shared practice in a community of people who are engaged in actions through a mutual interest. Facilitating interaction is an essential component of any practice; that is, being able to talk and interact while at work. Being in a community of practice does not mean that everybody believes in the same thing, but that practice is commonly negotiated. A community of practice may be shaped by external influences and conditions outside the control of its members, as a programme leader is by academic regulations and policies. However, the reality of programme leadership will be produced by participation within the resources and constraints of the situation.

Wenger (1999) recognised that people will belong to several communities of practice which can lead to problematic and permeable boundaries. The notion of constellations of practice refers to multiple communities of practice. The significance of the constellations of communities of practice is that they are interlinked, overlapping, or tied in some way. This adds to the complexity of viewing a single centripetal trajectory towards full participation. This is the reality of a programme leader who is likely to be fulfilling this role alongside others. Wenger (1999) identified other trajectories of participation, a peripheral trajectory either by choice or from necessity, are trajectories that never lead to full participation. If participation is on the periphery the individual may have less power to influence their domains and borders. An insider trajectory indicates that the formation of an identity does not end with full participation, suggesting that there is a movement within the community of practice as people's situation changes. A boundary trajectory spans boundaries and links communities of practice. This can be seen where programme leaders hold other roles within the university such as a departmental role. The final trajectory is an outbound one leading out of a community of practice such as when an individual is preparing for retirement or has an intention to leave their place of work, or role as programme leader.

The plethora of roles a programme leader has to keep in the air at the same time can sometimes feel like juggling and that a ball may drop at any moment. Programme leadership is a mammoth task that can be extremely challenging today. It can be a source of workplace stress.

Workplace stress

Workplace stress is a serious health and safety issue that has been recognised by the UK Health and Safety Executive (HSE). Areas identified as problematic are work demands, change, management support, and role clarity (HSE, 2021). Universities are no longer a low-stress place of work and concerns have been raised about the well-being of academics for over 20 years. Despite this timeframe, recent studies have shown there is still a problem, with psychological well-being scores remaining well below population norms (Fetherston et al., 2021). It is a global issue with research being undertaken in

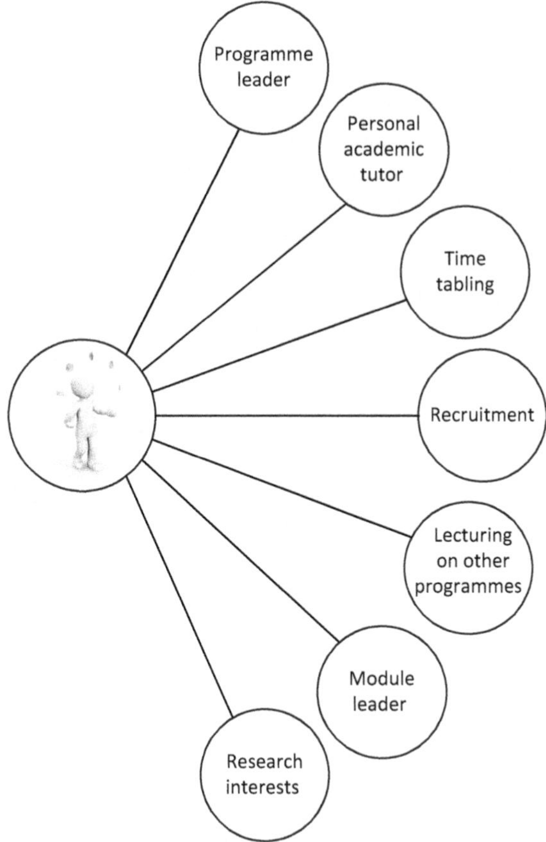

Figure 2.2 Juggling programme leader roles

several different countries including Australia (Bell et al., 2017), UK (Johnson et al., 2019), and Canada (Catano et al., 2010), Malaysia (Shaiful Azlan et al., 2017). Academics with responsibility for a programme may feel this more acutely.

Neo-liberal ideology has transformed the ethos of higher education since the nineties. There is a commodification of an academic's work and neo-liberal policy appears to benefit managers and focus on capital accumulation (Taberner, 2018). This has led to increased accountability of academics, particularly programme leaders, as focus on quality alongside increasing student numbers and pressure to publish research contribute to the stress of being an academic (Kinman, 2014; Bell et al., 2017). Other mounting pressures can be caused by widening participation, teaching internationally, alternative modes of delivery such as apprenticeship and online (Kinman, 2014; Bell et al., 2017). Increased financial pressures and rapid changes in working practices brought on by the Covid-19 pandemic have exacerbated these pre-existing issues. Jobs already at risk have become less secure and there is extensive use of temporary contracts (Taberner 2018). These rapid changes in practice with the increased use of digital technology and working from home mean that a programme leader can work, anytime, anyplace, anywhere. There is lots of flexibility in academic life, much of the work is not fixed by location allowing it to be highly portable to facilitate working in different venues, and at home. Working remotely can assist in managing competing demands; it can also result in conflicting emotions, feelings of guilt, and resentment (Kinman, 2014). It is not a panacea for addressing work–life conflict if the demands of the work outweigh the advantages of flexibility.

With the many demands on the programme leader, blurring of work and non-work in the lives of individuals, and the challenge of establishing a boundary between these domains can be challenging. The literature discusses this using different terms such as work–life balance, spill-over, work–life merge, work–life conflict, and blending. The issue is not only concerning time allocation and physical presence, it is also about focus, attention, and the personal investment in one of the domains at a detriment to the other. In their survey, Fetherston et al. (2021) found almost three-quarters of the Australian and UK academics reported intrusive work-related thoughts outside working hours. They also reported that a similar number of the respondents would check their work communications outside of work even though this was not necessary. Programme leaders often become absorbed in their work and this can lead to a blurring boundary between personal and professional life.

It is important not to ignore work-related stress as it can lead to burnout. This is prevalent in jobs that have intensive interaction with others and sustained emotional involvement as with the programme leader role (Watts and Robertson, 2011). Burnout with emotional exhaustion can have an adverse effect on classroom management and self-efficacy, and leads to the avoidance of pastoral care for students if feeling overburdened by the students' emotional needs (Watts and Robertson, 2011). Attempting to meet the needs of others can lead to emotional exhaustion which could result in academics distancing themselves emotionally as a form of protection (Kinman, 2014). There is a current drive to increase the prominence of personal academic tutors which can reduce the burden on programme leaders. However, it will expose more academic staff to significant interpersonal interaction, particularly with the increasing number of students, thus increasing their risk of burnout (Watts and Robertson, 2011). Other compounding factors impact on burnout, including role conflict, time pressures, conflicts with students, and student appraisal (Watts and Robertson, 2011). They also identified that younger staff appeared to be more vulnerable to burnout. This could be because older staff have developed more efficient coping mechanisms or that junior staff have more student contact hours.

On a positive note, even with high levels of stress and burnout among academics, the job can give high levels of satisfaction and academics find their work intrinsically motivating and rewarding (Kinman, 2014). Predictors of satisfaction include trust in management, autonomy procedural fairness, and a lack of work–life conflict (Kinman, 2014). If academics know about work stressors and their impacts it will enable them to act to minimise the effects of those stressors (Shaiful Azlan et al., 2017).

Key stressors

- Heavy workloads
- Extended working hours
- Poor work–life balance
- Increased student numbers
- Poor institutional communication
- Role ambiguity
- Pressure to publish
- Reductions in funding

Work–life balance

The programme leader role can give high levels of job satisfaction. Therefore having an understanding of work–life balance, you will be able to take steps to reduce the negative effects associated with the lack of a boundary between work and family domains, particularly when juggling conflicting demands. Although having separate periods of time for work and life activities is preferred by most people, some believe it is necessary to merge life and work activities in order to meet work demands (Fetherston et al., 2021). Even if a time-based border is in place spill-over may still occur from an emotional perspective (Clark, 2000).

It is both an organisational and individual responsibility to try to reduce the stress caused by poor work–life balance (Bell et al., 2017). Look at what help is available within your institution. Universities should offer programmes for employees to reduce work-related stress and support the achievement of work–life balance (Kinman, 2014; Bell et al., 2017). Examples include meditation classes, promoting exercise, planning and time-management skills sessions, and on building resilience (Bell et al., 2017). Performance management, anti-bullying and harassment policy, the recognition of excellence, increased social activities to raise morale and occupational health programmes are potential interventions for reducing work-related stress (Kinman, 2014).

Foster a good working relationship with your manager who has a role in supporting your work–life balance. Their management style should be one of respect and compassion. They should support you in managing your workload as well as managing relationships, for example dealing with conflict (Kinman, 2014). Whilst effectively managing respectfully and fairly they should also promote your autonomy as these can protect you from the negative effects of spill-over from work to home life (Kinman, 2014). Autonomy at work can be key to stress management. Top-down bureaucratic management cultures may promote a crisis of professional identity leading to low morale (Kinman, 2014).

Your team members can assist by sharing individual preferences for working patterns and how they achieve work–life balance. This enables team members to be sensitive to the preferences of others; for example, some people may be engaged in childcare at certain hours during the day and attend to work-related emails in the evening. However, one should not expect responses outside normal working hours, or use phrases that suggest this is the case. Role modelling and demonstrating effective personal work–life balance can be very effective for academics who are struggling to achieve this (Kinman, 2014).

As an individual you must take responsibility for your work–life balance, closely monitoring your workload and working hours. The programme leader role can eat away at your time; therefore, it is worthwhile undertaking a time and motion study, documenting how much time is spent on each activity to identify where changes can be made to your working practices. It is also useful to use theory to gain a greater understanding of the situation thus enabling creativity in finding novel strategies to reduce the conflict between work and home. One useful theory is the work/family border theory.

Work/family border theory

Work/family border theory goes somewhere way to explaining work–life conflict and thus how to obtain balance (Clark, 2000). It uses the analogy of people crossing borders between the world of work and the world of family. People can shape the worlds they are in and the borders between them. For many years workplaces and homes have been distinct from each other, separated physically, temporally, and with distinct cultures. This is no longer the case with modern society seeing working parents, families remote from social support and the drive for gender equality in the workplace. Spill-over theory recognises that despite physical and temporal boundaries behaviours and emotions from one world carry over into another thus the two worlds influence each other (Staines, 1980). These two worlds can be likened to different countries with different languages behaviours and cultures. As with countries, some differences are much greater than others, from those that are very similar to those that are quite polarised. Work/family border theory sees people as crossing the border, making transitions between the two worlds for example tailoring their language, behaviour, and goals. People can shape their worlds to some degree by adjusting borders and bridges to create an optimum balance.

The theory is built on the work of others such as Kurt Lewin's idea of life space and Lave and Wenger's communities of practice. The different world or domains have their own cultural expectations and priorities, workplaces are usually more formal hierarchical, and less intimate than family domains. The

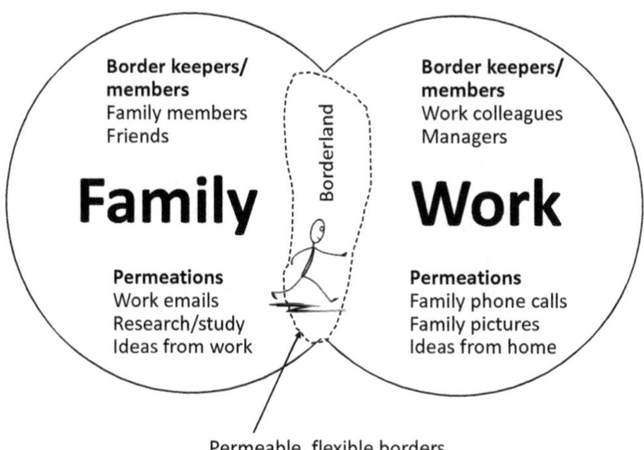

Figure 2.3 Work/family border theory

differences between the domains lay on a continuum from integration to complete segmentation, recognising that for some there is little distinction between work and home. For others, there is such a distinction that their whole persona changes. There is no ideal state of integration or segregation; people can find balance at all points on the continuum.

Work/family border theory sees a model balance when each domain provides essential but different needs. To look at how people achieve balance the idea of borders is explored. These are the lines of demarcation between domains: physical, temporal, and psychological. The physical border is the transition of the journey from work to home, which has currently been eroded as people are more often working from their homes. Temporal borders are set working hours, the divide when work is done, and family responsibility start. However, these have also been eroded as working from home means sometimes being interrupted by the needs of the family encroaching on work commitments and vice versa. Where physical and temporal borders may in the past have helped determine the psychological borders this is more challenging today.

The theory introduces the concept of permeability of the borders as the degree to which aspects of one domain enter another. There may, for example, be interruptions from the family domain such as being called by a family member whilst working which may have a negative impact. It can also be perceived positively, reminding the person that they are a member of another domain. Psychological permeation is more challenging if negative emotions spill over from one domain to another. However, positive spill-over is also possible as skills, creativity, and ideas from one domain can be transferred to another. The flexibility of the border relates to the extent to which the border can contract or expand depending on the demands of the domain. Borders can have a high degree of flexibility, particularly if working from home.

When there is permeability and flexibility between the domains blending occurs, creating what has been termed a borderland, an area that is not exclusively in one domain or the other. Blending can occur, for example, when thinking about a work problem whilst out walking the dogs. Residing in the borderland can be positive when blending personal and work experiences for mutual enrichment. It can be dangerous and uncomfortable when domains are very polarised. It is a place where conflict can arise with the need to juggle conflicting demands. It can be a place where there is unease about identity; for example, if a person's personality and behaviour change dramatically between the two domains. If the domains are similar blending can result in a sense of wholeness.

The strength of the border is determined by the degree of permeability, flexibility, and blending. There may be an imbalance in the strength of the border with the permeability or flexibility only going in one direction. For example, demands of work may see somebody working additional hours, but not to have the flexibility to take a time for carer's responsibilities when necessary. Domains and borders are to some extent self-created. This means that we need to look at the individual situation and how they can adjust their domains and borders for optimum balance. To facilitate this, it is useful to draw on the concept of participation in communities of practice.

Vignette

Since working from home my work–life balance has been better than ever. I have a chronic health condition and this flexibility allows me to intersperse work and home life. I can take breaks from sitting at my computer and do bits of housework or delay the start of my day if feeling tired in a morning. Before this move to home working my institution had an attitude of presenteeism. It required academics to be physically present in the university for a set time period. Sometimes I felt tied to my desk. In a communal office, I was aware of being on view. That people may make judgement on whether I was working hard enough or not.

As an educator, no one is going to automatically take over from me when I stop work, as is the case with shift work. What I don't do one day will still be there to do the next. So, I know I am keeping up with my workload, probably better than ever before. I feel happy and motivated.

I know it does not suit everyone but feel with this flexibility of working from home I have achieved an effective work–life balance, something which I haven't had for a long time!

Influence and identity

Programme leaders who have autonomy and flexibility to adjust their work and home can often have greater job satisfaction. If you have fully grasped the requirements of your role, i.e. a central participant of your domain, you are likely to have developed the ability to negotiate changes to your domain and its borders, thus achieve a balance between work and home.

An individual is more likely to spend time and energy on the domain it identifies most strongly with and on a role that holds the most meaning for them. If as a programme leader you internalise the values and practices of your domain (your programme) and your identity closely relates to that of the domain, your motivation to adjust borders and domains increases. A source of stress results if an individual identifies more strongly with one role than another as this threatens the balance. This can happen when you are fulfilling other roles alongside that of programme leader.

If you identify strongly with your domain and have a desire to shape and excel in that domain, you are likely to move towards central participation and be fully engaged with the role. Lack of identification with the role can lead to frustration and a gradual withdrawal from relationships with others in the domain.

Other people within your domain have a strong influence on defining the domain and its border. Work/family border theory identifies border keepers as members who have a role in border crossers' ability to manage their domains and borders. These could for example be managers or human resources departments within the institution. Work–life conflicts can occur when there is a disagreement between the border keeper and the border crosser on what constitutes each domain. At work, this can be things such as what constitutes time off in lieu or a carer's responsibilities. In the family domain, spouses may act as border keepers, carefully guarding their domain with the conflicts occurring, for example over the amount of time a person is spending on work activities at home.

Frequent effective communication between border keepers and border crossers is key to helping mutual understanding and reducing conflict.

Similarly, good communication with other members of a domain will develop awareness and understanding of the individual's situation. Work/family border theory talks about co-crossing where family members visit a workplace or where co-workers visit homes and get to know spouses. Support from other domains members, for example co-workers or spouses, can increase the well-being of the border crosser. Lack of understanding and support can increase the level of work–life conflict. Another thing that can have a negative impact is the characteristics of the domains. If values and cultures between home and work vary considerably it can lead to the boarder crosser living in two different worlds. This can make talking to co-workers about family, and family about work difficult, thus increasing work–life conflict.

Increased awareness and effective communication between domain members can facilitate flexibility required for work–life balance.

In summary, the tools identified by the work/family borders theory that facilitate work–life balance are as follows:

- Flexible working policies within an organisation make changes to the borders relatively easy.
- Having a similar culture between the family and work domains will facilitate work–life balance. If this is not possible then strong borders in both directions are needed to help an individual maintain balance.

- Having a strong supportive relationship between the individual and the border keeper of a domain, i.e. a line manager, should aid work–life balance.
- Central participation in a domain, with an individual strongly identifying with their domain, empowers that individual to develop their work–life balance.
- Communication and developing supportive relationships with co-workers can create greater understanding which can be used to gain a better work–life balance.
- Central participation at both work and home will result in developing expertise in the areas of responsibility. If roles become an integral part of a person's identity it will reduce conflict.

Reflection

Using the work/family border theory as a platform, reflect on your work–life balance.

Consider your domains.

Are you a central participant?

Can you identify any communities of practice on which you are on the periphery?

If so, is this where you feel most comfortable? How could you move towards being a central participant?

Consider your relationships within the domains.

How is your relationship with your line manager?

Do they understand your personal circumstances? How can they help you improve your work–life balance?

How can your co-workers support you in achieving an optimum work–life balance?

How much do you share your work experiences with people in your family domain?

Think about the values and cultures of the domains in which you reside.

Is there a close alignment between the domains?

Are there any aspects that cause friction?

Think about your borders.

Are both borders equally flexible and permeable?

If one is stronger than the other what can you do to address this?

To what extend to you know and use flexible working policies at your institution?

Emotional labour

Programme leaders experience pressure from neo-liberal policies that put attention on customer service, viewing students as consumers (Lawless, 2018). Widening participation, marketisation, and the prestige economy all sculpt your relationship with students (Berry and Cassidy, 2013). Effectively higher education has become a service industry, and it has been shown that emotional labour is high in the human service industry (Lawless, 2018). Academics are increasingly being involved in pastoral care (Berry and Cassidy, 2013). The expectations of students particularly in being nurtured and cared for may be beyond your capacity as programme leader (Chowdhry, 2014). This can cause feelings of frustration but demonstrating anger or frustration to the students is inappropriate.

Emotional labour is the effort required to display perceived expected emotions (Ogbonna and Harris, 2004). It can be associated with workplace stress which may manifest as feeling robotic, un-empathetic, emotional exhaustion, and cynicism (Berry and Cassidy, 2013). There are unwritten emotional expectations for individuals working in higher education (Lawless, 2018). This means that academics are required to suppress their own emotions in order to display the ones expected (Berry and Cassidy, 2013). Hochschild (1979) was a pioneer in developing an understanding of emotion in the workplace. The concept includes pointing out a difference between *surface acting* and *deep acting*. Acting is a way of managing one's emotions to produce a visual display aimed at influencing the emotions of others. Surface acting is pretending to feel an emotion whereas deep acting is using memories or imagination to evoke the emotion that is displayed. According to Hochschild (1983) there is a strain caused when pretending to feel emotions that are not actually felt.

Programme leaders of care courses are particularly susceptible to emotional labour as they are likely to have had many years of experience in their caring profession where care and compassion are considered central to the role, thus, making it challenging to form the boundary between caring and ensuring the requirements of the programme are met (Chowdhry, 2014). Literature also suggests links between gender and levels of emotional labour, with females being more susceptible (Chowdhry, 2014; Lawless, 2018). This is steeped in historical culture beyond the scope of this book but it is an interesting concept as it is linked to mothering and homemaker, women performing emotional unpaid work (Lawless, 2018). It has been shown that younger and less experienced academics can display higher levels of emotional labour (Berry and Cassidy, 2013). As a programme leader the need to 'keep your emotions in check' could possibly extend to more than with students. It may be frustrating at times dealing with other people who contribute to the programme.

Even with the formal student support structures within higher education academics, especially programme leaders will inevitably have a welfare role. Students will disclose their personal problems and it may be hard not to be drawn into becoming involved. Whilst caring is becoming part of a programme leader role it is not forming part of your training (Lawless, 2018). When leading on a professional programme there is an expectation that you will display the values and behaviours of your profession. For example, if leading on a healthcare programme you will display the values in accordance with your professional codes of conduct (Chowdhry, 2014). Programme leaders may try to altruistically give care to students in the same way that they would give to patients. This can feel overwhelming by the sheer volume of students involved as you try to convey to students that you have time for them but in the back of your mind there is a multitude of other things that you have to do. You hide your frustrations and greet students with a smile.

Surface acting will be used to hide an academic's frustration from students until there is the opportunity to vent their feelings outside the classroom. This venting of feelings is something that can be observed in staff meetings with colleagues being used as a source of informal support. Having a private space in which to relax is important. Some universities have an open-door office policy. The story of one of the participants interviewed in the large qualitative study by Ogbonna and Harris (2004) will resonate with many academics as they described how they were just starting to relax when there was a knock on the door, and they spent the next 20 minutes smiling at a student whilst screaming inside.

You should start to recognise emotional labour as something that contributes to your work as a programme leader. Think about how the move to seeing the student as a customer has impacted on your work as programme leader. Have office hours been extended, are you on-call via email, are you are on hand to deal with the plethora of student emergencies (Lawless, 2018)? One thing that would help with this is to count the amount of time spent communicating with students both during and outside office hours. Institutions need to recognise that this affective work needs doing. However, it is often hidden work, therefore taking time to document the time spent answering emails or talking to a distressed student helps to acknowledge this emotional and temporal labour (Berry and Cassidy, 2013). To help raise awareness, Lawless (2018) suggests talking to students about our workload. Collective visibility about emotional labour may help to inform academic workloads, your own expectations, and those of your organisation and students (Lawless, 2018).

Vignette

One of the tasks associated with being a programme leader is that of disciplining students for breaching academic or professional regulations. Personally, I would liken the experience of undertaking a disciplinary hearing a bit like going into court!

The weeks prior to a panel hearing were incredibly time-consuming, completing paperwork, ascertaining all the facts, and ensuring that I knew my case inside and out. I knew who, what, why, when, where, and how. I ensured that I followed the disciplinary procedure to the letter, as I knew any case could easily be dismissed.

Once I was in the panel hearing, I found that it was not the behaviour of the student being called into question; instead, it was my methods that were scrutinised. I found myself defending my actions as programme leader and found panels to be overly sympathetic to the behaviours of the student.

Throughout the disciplinary process, the student has access to support via the Union of Students. In many cases, the student representative will accompany a student to the panel hearing. As for support for a PL, I received little to no support preparing or undertaking disciplinary procedures; it was a lonely process.

I found the outcomes of these hearings to be incredibly emotionally frustrating and draining. You are defending the university and/or your profession and I often found that the outcomes and indeed penalties imposed were not reflective of the crime! I think it is at times like these when I recognised the 'power of the student' and, to be honest, in my disappointment I questioned the value of pursuing any student via a disciplinary process.

Ultimately, I have to make my peace that I will continue to follow the procedure, build a solid case, and accept that in all likelihood I won't get the outcome I desire. That said, I will keep going – one day it might just go my way.

Compassion fatigue

As a programme leader, you may be exposed to another's suffering; for example, interacting with distressed or disappointed students. Compassion fatigue is considered a 'cost of caring'; it is an empathetic reaction after being exposed to another's suffering (Figley, 2002). Empathy is the ability to emotionally resonate with a person (Huggard, 2004). Direct exposure to the emotional energy of somebody who is suffering elicits an empathetic reaction. As a programme leader, you may project yourself into the perspective of the student and experience anger, frustration, or other emotions the student may be experiencing. The accumulation of emotional energy resulting from an empathetic response can cause compassion fatigue. Counteracting this, you may feel a sense of achievement at being able to help find a successful outcome for the student (Levkovich and Ricon, 2020).

In the programme leader role, long-term exposure to students' trauma can potentially initiate an emotional response leading to burnout. Burnout is generally associated with workplace stressors such as workload and working conditions. It is a process in which an academic will gradually lose interest in their work, become depleted, and lack enthusiasm (Levkovich and Ricon, 2020). Burnout via compassion fatigue is from stressors experienced through relationships for example with students or colleagues (Boyle, 2015). There has been increased interest in the concept of compassion fatigue primarily within health and social care providers, but also in other fields such as counselling (Sinclair et al., 2017; Levkovich and Ricon, 2020). Kinnick et al., (1996) explored this concept in the general public concerning societal problems. Compassion fatigue has been described as secondary traumatic stress (Figley, 2002) or emotional burnout (Kinnick et al., 1996). Secondary trauma is a process occurring to a person who is not directly exposed to trauma but identifies with the victim and develops secondary post-traumatic symptoms as a result of indirect exposure (Levkovich and Ricon, 2020.

Compassion fatigue linked with emotional burnout can manifest as tiredness, depression, anger, apathy, and detachment, with physical manifestations of headaches, insomnia, and gastrointestinal conditions (Sinclair et al., 2017). Psychological symptoms may be emotional exhaustion, negative self-image, or depression. A person might become short-tempered or resentful of their situation (Boyle, 2015). As a coping mechanism, programme leaders may find themselves distancing from students and avoiding interaction (Kinnick et al., 1996). Compassion fatigue may result in desensitisation or reduced feelings of sympathy or empathy (Kinnick et al., 1996). Cynicism, resentment, and a dread of working directly with students may also start to materialise (Sinclair et al, 2017). As a means of emotional self-protection, a programme leader could find themselves withdrawing or disengaging from emotionally charged situations, for example academic conduct meetings with students (Kinnick et al., 1996; Huggard, 2004; Boyle, 2015; Levkovich and Ricon, 2020).

There are a variety of recommended interventions; these include self-care and well-being programmes from within the institution. The development of personal qualities such as resilience (the ability to cope with or overcome exposure to adversity) and self-awareness are also recommended (Huggard, 2004; Sinclair et al., 2017). Self-care includes such interventions as exercise, nutrition, and a healthy lifestyle. There are also other activities to promote relaxation such as art, mindfulness, and yoga (Boyle, 2015). Healthy social networks and interacting with other programme leaders or colleagues who can offer emotional support, role models, and mentors can also be very valuable ways of combating compassion fatigue. Debriefing, commonly used within healthcare, is a way of discharging pent-up emotion. You may need to establish well-defined boundaries and practise responsible selfishness to reduce the risk of compassion fatigue (Boyle, 2015).

Vignette

I was programme leader for an undergraduate programme with nearly one hundred students on the programme. This was a time before the introduction of personal academic tutors and even though there were central student support services, all student issues that impacted on their academic performance would come through me as programme leader. These issues included a range of anxiety, stressful experiences on placement, family bereavements, and challenging domestic situations. I found myself regularly listening to students divulging their circumstances, often whilst in a high emotional state. This is something for which I was untrained and unprepared. I found myself absorbing their emotions in what I now recognise as a form of secondary traumatic stress. I found myself mulling over their situation in the evening or waking up in the early hours of the morning thinking about things. I recognised I was in a downward spiral of depression, not from my own situation but from listening to other people's distressing stories.

It took only one session with a counsellor to start me on a healthier pathway. I took three pieces of advice from that session:

1 They are not my children; I do not need to 'mother' them and it is not my role to 'fix' things for them.
2 Keep a diary and write down in it anything that is still on my mind at the end of the working day and anything that I need to do the next day. This helps to 'park' any thoughts that can be picked up the next day.
3 Have a closing down routine to both physically and mentally form a boundary between work and home life. For example, writing in my diary, closing the computer, and tidying my desk.

I have applied this advice throughout my continued working life, and it has helped me to develop into a healthier programme leader.

Summary

Programme leaders have numerous, potentially conflicting roles to fulfil. The plethora of roles a programme leader has to keep in the air at the same time can sometimes feel like juggling and that a ball may drop at any moment. The main support available for programme leaders from various universities is information about the roles and responsibilities of programme leadership, of which there are many. Various programme leader courses do exist, some within institutions and others from external organisations. These generally cover curriculum design, learning and teaching approaches, organisation of a programme, and pedagogy. Peer support can be an invaluable mechanism that will help you fulfil your role as programme leader. There is value in sharing experiences with other programme leaders, as long as this is in a non-threatening environment. Moral support from colleagues can help you build self-confidence. Mentoring can also be a valuable source of support for programme leaders. This chapter provided ideas on how to get the most out of a mentoring relationship. Networking via programme leader forums can be a valuable source of support. This chapter acknowledged that programme leaders can be susceptible to workplace stress. This is exacerbated by increasing student numbers, widening participation, and the consumerist approach to higher education. Particularly with new ways of working the blurring of work and non-work in the lives of programme leaders is likely and can lead to work-related stress. This chapter discussed issues faced by programme leaders in terms of their well-being and support and provided strategies for being a healthy programme leader.

References

Advance HE, 2021. Enhancing programme leadership. Available from https://www.advance-he.ac.uk/programmes-events/development-programmes/enhancing-programme-leadership (accessed 4 October 2021).

Bell, A.S., Rajendran, D. and Theiler, S., 2012. Job stress, wellbeing, work–life balance and work-life conflict among Australian academics. *E-Journal of Applied Psychology*, 8(1), pp. 25–37.

Berry, K.E. and Cassidy, S.F., 2013. Emotional labour in university lecturers: Considerations for higher education institutions. *Journal of Curriculum and Teaching*, 2(2), pp. 22–36.

Boud, D. and Middleton, H., 2003. Learning from others at work: Communities of practice and informal learning. *Journal of Workplace Learning*, 15(5), pp. 194–202. doi:10.1108/13665620310483895

Boyle, D.A., 2015. Compassion fatigue: The cost of caring. *Nursing2020*, 45(7), pp. 48–51.

Bruner, J.S., 1996. *The culture of education*. Harvard University Press.

Bruner, J.S., Goodnow, J.J., and Austin, G.A., 1956. A study of thinking. Wiley.

Cahill, J., Bowyer, J., Rendell, C., Hammond, A. and Korek, S., 2015. An exploration of how programme leaders in higher education can be prepared and supported to discharge their roles and responsibilities effectively. *Educational Research*, 57(3), pp. 272–286.

Carmel, R.G. and Paul, M.W., 2015. Mentoring and coaching in academia: Reflections on a mentoring/coaching relationship. *Policy Futures in Education*, 13(4), pp. 479–491.

Catano, V., Francis, L., Haines, T., Kirpalani, H., Shannon, H., Stringer, B., and Lozanzki, L., 2010. Occupational stress in Canadian universities: A national survey. *International Journal of Stress Management*, 17(3), pp. 232–258.

Chenot, David, Benton, Amy D. and Kim, H., 2009. The influence of supervisor support, peer support, and organizational culture among early career social workers in child welfare services. *Child Welfare*, 88 (5), pp. 129–147.

Chowdhry, S., 2014. The caring performance and the 'blooming student': Exploring the emotional labour of further education lecturers in Scotland. *Journal of Vocational Education & Training*, 66(4), pp. 554–571.

Clark, S.C., 2000. Work/family border theory: A new theory of work/family balance. *Human relations*, 53(6), pp. 747–770.

Daniels, H., 2005. *An introduction to Vygotsky.* Routledge.

Ellis, S. and Nimmo, A. 2018. Opening eyes and changing mind-sets: professional development for programme leaders. In J. Lawrence and S. Ellis (eds), *Supporting programme leaders and programme leadership.* Staff and Educational Development Association, SEDA Special London.

Eraut, M., 2000. Non-formal learning and tacit knowledge in professional work. *British Journal of Educational Psychology*, 70(1), pp. 113–136.

Eraut, M., 2007. Learning from other people in the workplace. *Oxford Review of Education*, 33(4), pp. 403–422.

Fetherston, C., Fetherston, A., Batt, S., Sully, M., and Wei, R., 2021. Wellbeing and work–life merge in Australian and UK academics. *Studies in Higher Education*, 46 (12), pp. 2774–2788.

Figley, C.R., 2002. Compassion fatigue: Psychotherapists' chronic lack of self care. *Journal of Clinical Psychology*, 58(11), pp. 1433–1441.

Fleer, M., 1990. Scaffolding conceptual change in early childhood. *Research in Science Education*, 20(1), pp. 114–123.

Health and Safety Executive, 2021. Work-related stress. Available from https://www.hse.gov.uk/stress/ (accessed 4 October 2021).

Hochschild, A.R., 1979. Emotion work, feeling rules, and social structure. *American Journal of Sociology*, 85(3), pp. 551–575.

Hochschild, A.R., 1983. *The managed heart.* University of California Press.

Huggard, P., 2004. Compassion fatigue: How much can I give? In S. Barrett, C. Komaromy, M. Robb, and A. Rogers (eds), *Communication, relationships and care* (pp. 204–207). Routledge.

Johnson, S.J., Willis, S.M., and Evans, J., 2019. An examination of stressors, strain, and resilience in academic and non-academic UK university job roles. *International Journal of Stress Management*, 26(2), pp. 162–172.

Kinman, G. 2014. Doing more with less? Work and wellbeing in academics. *Somatechnics*, 4(2), pp. 219–235.

Kinman, G. and Jones, F., 2004. Running up the down escalator: Stressors and strains in UK academics. *Quality Control and Applied Statistics*, 49(4), pp. 439–442.

Kinman, G., and Wray, S. 2013. *Higher stress: A survey of stress and well-being among staff in higher education.* University and College Union.

Kinnick, K.N., Krugman, D.M., and Cameron, G.T., 1996. Compassion fatigue: Communication and burnout toward social problems. *Journalism & Mass Communication Quarterly*, 73(3), pp. 687–707.

Knippelmeyer, S.A. and Torraco, R.J., 2007. *Mentoring as a developmental tool for higher education.* Paper presented at the Academy of Human Resource

Development International Research Conference in The Americas (Indianapolis, IN, 28 February–4 March)

Lave, J. and Wenger, E., 1991. *Situated learning: Legitimate peripheral participation*. Cambridge University Press.

Lawless, B., 2018. Documenting a labor of love: Emotional labor as academic labor. *Review of Communication*, 18(2), pp. 85–97.

Levkovich, I. and Ricon, T., 2020. Understanding compassion fatigue, optimism and emotional distress among Israeli school counsellors. *Asia Pacific Journal of Counselling and Psychotherapy*, 11(2), pp. 159–180.

Morton-Cooper, A. and Palmer, A., 1999. *Mentoring, preceptorship and clinical supervision: A guide to clinical support and supervision*. Blackwell Science.

Ogbonna, E. and Harris, L.C., 2004. Work intensification and emotional labour among UK university lecturers: An exploratory study. *Organization Studies*, 25(7), pp. 1185–1203.

Parker, P., Hall, D.T., and Kram, K.E., 2008. Peer coaching: A relational process for accelerating career learning. *Academy of Management Learning & Education*, 7(4), pp. 487–503.

Siegel, P., 2000. Using peer mentors during periods of uncertainty. *Leadership & Organization Development Journal*, 21(5), pp. 243–253.

Sinclair, S., Raffin-Bouchal, S., Venturato, L., Mijovic-Kondejewski, J., and Smith-MacDonald, L., 2017. Compassion fatigue: A meta-narrative review of the healthcare literature. *International Journal of Nursing Studies*, 69, pp. 9–24.

Shaiful Azlan, K., Rosnah, I., and Rizal Mohd, A.M., 2017. Systematic review of organization stressors as predictors for job stress and burnout among university academicians in Malaysia. *International Journal of Public Health and Clinical Sciences*, 4(3), pp. 35–46.

Smidt, S., 2009. *Introducing Vygotsky: A guide for practitioners and students in the early years*. Routledge.

Solomon, P., 2004, Peer support/peer provided services underlying processes, benefits, and critical ingredients. *Psychiatric Rehabilitation Journal*, 27 (4), pp. 392–401.

Staff and Educational Development Association, 2021. Supporting and leading educational change. Available from https://www.seda.ac.uk/ (accessed 4 October 2021).

Staines, G.L., 1980. Spillover versus compensation: A review of the literature on the relationship between work and nonwork. *Human relations*, 33(2), pp. 111–129.

Taberner, A.M., 2018. The marketisation of the English higher education sector and its impact on academic staff and the nature of their work. *International Journal of Organizational Analysis*, 26(1), pp. 129–152.

Turner, R., Huang, R., Poverjuc, O., and Wyness, L., 2016. What role do teaching mentors play in supporting new university lecturers to develop their teaching practices? *Professional Development in Education*, 42(4), pp. 647–665.

Vygotsky, L.S. and Cole, M., 1978. *Mind in society: The development of higher psychological processes*. Harvard University Press.

Watts, J. and Robertson, N., 2011. Burnout in university teaching staff: A systematic literature review. *Educational Research*, 53(1), pp. 33–50.

Wenger, E., 1999. *Communities of practice: Learning, meaning, and identity*. Cambridge University Press.

3 Quality

Background to quality in higher education

The Conservative government under Margaret Thatcher made radical changes to the public sector including higher education. The Jarratt report (1985) saw the move to students being viewed as customers introducing a competitive nature between institutions. Neo-liberal ideals such as marketisation require universities to act like businesses. The idea of students as customers was reinforced by the Education (Students Loans) Act 1990 which enabled eligible students to receive loans towards their maintenance (United Kingdom Government, 1990). The white paper Higher Education Meeting the Challenge (1987) set out the difficulties in funding and a revised policy on access to higher education. It emphasised the need for quality and efficiency acknowledging that quality could not be imposed from outside but stating that the government would be seeking to ensure that quality systems were in place and began monitoring the results (Her Majesty's Stationery Office, 1987). Quality was to be judged on four main areas: academic standards, the quality of teaching, the achievement of students, and the quality of research. The white paper preceded the Education Reform Act 1988. This act brought about the abolition of academic tenure, an indefinite academic appointment, thus removing some academic freedom. The act was extended to the Further and Higher Education Act 1992 making changes to the funding and administration of both further and higher education. This opened the doors to polytechnics becoming universities, sometimes known as new universities or post-1992 universities. It also made it a legal requirement for funding councils to establish a committee to assess quality in higher education (Harvey 2005).

Higher education policy becomes increasingly neo-liberal and shapes quality assurance within the sector. By the 1990s quality, linked to funding, had become a prominent concern within UK higher education (Harvey, 2005). The Dearing report (1997) Higher Education and Learning Society set out a vision for higher education for the following 20 years. This had a significant impact on funding for higher education, with the introduction of student fees. It also promoted widening participation, and had an impact on institutional governance, setting out recommendations for the Higher Education Funding

DOI: 10.4324/9781003126355-4

Council to England (HEFCE) and the Quality Assurance Agency (QAA). The QAA, established in 1997, is an independent body for providing quality assurance in higher education which developed a set of benchmarks for quality and standards. The Education and Research Act 2017 replaced the Further and Higher Education Act 1992 and saw the establishment of the Office for Students in England, which was given the responsibility of regulating the higher education sector, replacing the HEFCE and the Office for Fair Access. In England, Office for Students grants degree-awarding powers, and the right for providers to use 'university' in their title. The act has a detailed section on quality and standards, giving power to the Office for Students to assess the quality of higher education provided by English higher education providers. In Scotland, Wales, and Northern Ireland applications for degree awarding powers go via their relevant government to the QAA.

Quality assurance

The revised UK Quality Code for Higher Education (Quality Assurance Agency, 2018) sets out a series of expectations for demonstrating effective quality assurance. This was a joint publication from the UK standing committee for quality assessment (UKSCQA) and the QAA. The UKSCQA works to promote student interests and provides oversight of higher education quality assessment arrangements across the UK. The code has three elements: setting out expectations, expressing the outcomes that providers should achieve, and practices that represent the effective ways of working to meet the expectations and deliver positive outcomes to students. The code provides advice and guidance for developing and maintaining effective quality assurance practices. It is important to note that funders, regulators, and the QAA will use the code as a basis for assessing the quality of a higher education provision. The code covers aspects of admissions, delivery, facilities, student engagement, student complaints and appeals, partnership arrangements, and student support. These practices sit within the role of programme leader who will play a key role in meeting the standards and in evidencing that expectations for standards and quality are being met.

The teaching excellence and student outcomes framework (TEF) was introduced by the UK government in 2017 and is undergoing review in 2021 (Office for Students, 2021a). Its aim is to assess the quality of teaching at universities and colleges that provide higher education. The awards are divided into gold, silver, bronze, and provisional. The awards are judged by independent panels consisting of students, academics, and employer representatives. The scheme is voluntary but in England there is a link to tuition fees allowing providers to charge a higher rate if they have a TEF award. At present, the awards are only applicable to undergraduate teaching; however, they will have a knock-on effect on postgraduate teaching as initiatives introduced to improve undergraduate programmes are likely to be applied to other programmes in an institution. The scheme is continuously evolving, providing a resource to assist students in their decision about where to go to university. The areas examined include teaching quality, the learning environment, and the outcomes achieved by students. Data from other sources such as the National Student Survey (NSS) and Graduate Outcomes survey are used to inform submissions for the awards. It is very important for you to engage with the NSS if you are programme leader for an undergraduate programme in the UK. The results of the survey are made publicly available and influence the decisions prospective students make. They are published both on the Discover Uni website (2021) and the Office for Students website (2021b). TEF does not rank or compare institutions as with league tables. The awards are achieved through meeting quality standards. The type of award does have implications for the public image of the institution as the awards are used in advertising, and on tuition fees in England. The quantification of quality is a debated point. Marketisation of higher education means that metrics, analytics, and ranking will be around for a long time. As a programme leader, you will be required to engage in these processes. To do this you need to be aware of the aspects on which institutions are assessed.

The National Student Survey is open to all final-year undergraduate students for feedback on the whole of their programme. This is commissioned by the Office for Students, the Department for Economy Northern Ireland, the Higher Education Funding Council for Wales, and the Scottish Funding Council. It relates to eight aspects of the student experience.

1 Teaching on the course
2 Learning opportunities
3 Assessment and feedback
4 Academic support
5 Organisation and management
6 Learning resources
7 Learning community
8 Student voice

The responses need to meet a publication threshold of 50 per cent response rate and at least 10 students. The survey forms a key component of quality review. As such a programme leader of an undergraduate programme will be required to engage in the processes of encouraging students to complete the survey in order to meet the threshold for publication, analysing and responding to the results, and producing an action plan for improvement. Drops in percentages need to be scrutinised and explained, comparisons will be made with previous years and with other programmes. Programme leaders of postgraduate programmes do not escape scrutiny. The Advance HE Postgraduate Taught Experience Survey (PTES) provides a benchmark against other providers and can give insight into enhancements needed for learning and teaching. PTES, first piloted in 2009, looks at the following areas:

- Teaching and learning
- Engagement
- Assessment and feedback
- Organisation and management
- Skills development

It is not unheard of for programme leaders to find themselves in meetings with senior managers having to explain the results of such surveys for their programme. Thus, ignoring the process and leaving it to chance is not the best approach. You should engage with the process and below are some suggestions on how this can be done:

- Have a planned approach to publicising the surveys. One thing to consider is the timing of deployment. For example, asking the students to complete the survey when students are dispersed at different placements may not yield the best response rate. Most universities will have an institutional wide plan for promoting the NSS including incentives such as giving money to charity based on the number of responses.
- Students are often inundated with emails. It is useful to warn them to expect a link to the survey and highlight the importance of completing it. You cannot coach or instruct students on how to respond to the surveys, but you can discuss the benefits of completing the survey and how you use the data. The use of inappropriate influence may be investigated by the funding bodies. You should encourage students to take a well-rounded view of their experience rather than a reactive response following a recent assignment or teaching experience. It will help students to do this if you have provided a variety of mechanisms for them to give feedback throughout the programme.
- Be open and transparent about how the responses to national surveys are acted on. Discuss and share with students the responses and actions from previous years. Get students involved in developing action plans for the enhancement of the programme based on previous responses. When devising action plans focus on long-term strategies rather than quick fixes.

External expertise

The Quality Code requires programmes to have guidance from external impartial and independent expertise. The QAA (2018) provides advice and guidance on external expertise. This includes external examiners, external advisors, professional, statutory, and regulatory bodies (PRSBs), external stakeholders and speakers, and students. An external examiner system is a form of external quality monitoring that has been around since the nineteenth century. Over the years it has come under scrutiny and review but still currently forms part of the quality assurance in higher education (QAA, 2018). Programme leaders will be most familiar with external examiners in a moderating role. However, increasingly external examiners form part of the planning and review process. Advance HE (2019) has published a comprehensive handbook for external examiners which programme leaders might find useful for familiarising themselves with the role. An external examiner can act as a critical friend. As with any friendship, it is important for you as programme leader to strengthen and foster that relationship. Institutions will normally have a department responsible for external examiners including running induction events, and there may be standards of practice around sharing information with external examiners. You will need to become familiar with both the institution's practices and with your external examiner's expectations. These may vary in such things as a point of contact. Some external examiners are happy for each module leader to contact them whilst others prefer a single point of contact. Whatever arrangements are made there should be clear lines of communication. It is useful to have documentation all in one convenient place. The types of information they require are as follows:

- The assessment schedules
- Assessment guidelines and marking schemes
- Module descriptors and assessment criteria
- The composition, expectations, and timing of the assessment boards
- Assessment regulations
- Programme specifications

Expectations around the external moderation of assessments may vary; for example, some institutions do not require external moderation of assessments which do not contribute to a student's degree classification. You should discuss and clarify with your external examiner the method adopted for accessing samples of students' work and what that sample should be. If practicable external examiners are encouraged to meet some of the students on the programme to gain greater insight into the students' experience. It is the role of the external examiner to moderate, providing feedback on an assessment as it is set, and checking for overall accuracy and fairness against a marking criterion. It is not within their remit to adjust individual students' marks. They can, however, provide independent advice around scaling up or scaling down of an entire cohort. An external examiner will submit an annual report to which the programme leader should respond. These are objective reports on the standard and quality of the programme which can be used to inform quality enhancement.

Engaging with the student body and other stakeholders

Engaging with students and other stakeholders is an essential aspect of quality assurance. They provide a platform for monitoring and reviewing the quality of the programme. These should be regular and well-documented events and can include formal mechanisms such as staff–student committee, student representative, and placement provider meetings. The way to run a programme that gains high satisfaction is by constantly reviewing and reflecting using a variety of platforms to obtain feedback rather than waiting for an end of programme review. It is important to engage with not only the students but with all stakeholders. Below details some of the methods that can be used.

The student's voice

The student's voice plays an important role in contributing to the quality of your programme. Some institutions will have structures in place to support and facilitate student representation from your programme. Students should be elected from within a cohort; quite often they are volunteers, sometimes the only volunteers, therefore no actual election is needed. It is good practice for the student representative to be elected and accepted by the rest of the cohort. Once elected to the position this individual will need guidance on their role. This may come centrally from within the organisation and/or from the Union of Students. They will need guidance on how to truly represent the views of their cohort, methods of how to gather those views, and how to conduct themselves within a formal meeting setting.

As the programme leader, you can use this student rep system to gain valuable feedback and as a mechanism of distributing information to the rest of the cohort. Student reps may come with their own feedback from the cohort or you may ask them for targeted feedback on a particular aspect of the programme. Virtual or face-to-face meetings can be arranged between the programme leader and the student reps or be more inclusive with the whole programme delivery team. Sometimes a richer depth of discussion can be had in the more private session just with a programme leader, particularly if there is an issue with a particular module or member of staff. A small student rep meeting with the programme leader prior to a larger more formal meeting can be useful to iron out any small niggles before airing them to a wider audience. This does not mean that you intend to quash any of the issues, but you can help to prioritise what is important to raise in a wider platform, be forewarned about any issues they are likely to raise, and possibly respond to or resolve some of the issues.

Staff–student committee meetings

Student committee meetings tend to be a formal platform for gaining feedback from different stakeholders. These may include representation from students, placement providers, experts in the field, student support services, and the programme delivery team. You will likely have a core group of people whom you regularly invite, and additional people may be invited to specific meetings; for example, someone from admissions or quality. These are formal meetings quite often chaired by the programme leader who may or may not have administrative support. For an academic, particularly if they have come from industry, this may be the first experience of chairing a meeting. These meetings can be a valuable networking opportunity, gathering informal information by chatting with attendees both before and after the meeting. It is useful therefore to schedule this time into your diary, rather than just the time of the actual meeting.

Organising and chairing a meeting

Formal quality meetings are often part of an internal quality structure and include formal agenda and administrative support. As a new programme leader, it may be your first encounter at organising and chairing a formal meeting, which can be quite daunting.

The organisation of a meeting is sometimes undertaken by administrative colleagues, but it might be within the programme leader role. Even with the assistance of an administrator, they may come to you to find out what you want in the meeting and how you would like it to run. Your aim as chair of the meeting is to manage the timekeeping making sure that the meeting starts and finishes on time. You also need to make sure that all the items are discussed and that everyone's views have been heard. There should also be outcomes from the meeting with a clear action assigned to individuals or groups. The vignette below provides some practical tips.

Vignette

My first experience of chairing a formal meeting was a programme committee meeting. This included representatives from senior management, external partners, students, support services, and academics. There are several steps to chairing: before, during, and after the meeting. Here are some practical considerations for chairing a meeting.

Before the meeting

Think about what you want to get out of the meeting and what format it will take. For example, it may be useful to have a short presentation at the start of the meeting.

Information will need distributing before the meeting. This will include the agenda, minutes from the previous meeting, and any reports you would like people to read in preparation. There are practical considerations such as whether to provide refreshments. If it is a virtual meeting you need to ensure that participants know how to join and have the technology to be able to do so.

It helps with planning the meeting to ask for items for inclusion prior to setting the agenda. If you do not have administrative support, identify someone to take notes as it is difficult to both chair a meeting and to document it. Both virtual and face-to-face meetings can be recorded if the participants agree.

During the meeting

You want attendees to feel comfortable and contribute to the discussion. To do this start by welcoming them and have everyone introduce themselves with their name and role if numbers allow. You should receive any apologies for absence. It may also be necessary to check for any conflict of interest on agenda items.

Introduce the format and ground rules for the meeting. Attending a programme committee meeting is a good development opportunity for student representatives. Some students may be comfortable in this environment, but for others this may be a very new experience. Ground rules can include:

- asking people to speak through the chair by putting their hand up if they wished to speak – many virtual platforms also have the facility to raise a hand;
- not interrupting other people;
- not talking amongst themselves;
- respecting other people's views.

You are in charge of the meeting and you may need to remind people of the rules if they start to chat amongst themselves or want to continue talking about a previous agenda item when you have moved on. It is important in the meeting that you hear everybody's views. This can be particularly challenging if there is a perceived difference in the hierarchy. You may need to restrain anyone who is talking too much and encourage anyone who is quiet, nervous, or new to attending a meeting.

Chairing a meeting is about being vigilant. Look for people's body language that indicates they would like to say something. You could encourage attendees by specifically asking them directly. Some people prefer to sit back and listen before making any contribution. So, it is useful to ask if anyone has any further thoughts on an issue before moving on to the next item on the agenda. In a small meeting, you could go around each person in turn asking for their views; this is not practical in larger meetings. Before moving on to the next agenda item, it is useful to briefly summarise the discussion and state any actions or decisions that have been made.

Some meetings can be challenging; for example, with attendees who like the sound of their own voice, who feel that their opinion is the only right one. If you have two people who feel strongly about an issue it might lead to a heated debate. If this happens take control of the situation, asking them politely to be quiet for a little while, and ask somebody else in the meeting for their contribution.

Close the meeting by summarising the action points and letting the attendees know if and when any future meetings will take place. It is also good practice to let them know when the meeting notes will be available and distributed and thank people for attending.

After the meeting

Meetings can provide a good networking opportunity so consider allowing time after the meeting for this. You should have action notes from the meeting to circulate to the attendees.

Gathering wider feedback

Consultation via representation is valuable but has its limitations. There is a danger of only obtaining the strongest views of the few. It is therefore important to engage on a more individual basis. A variety of methods for obtaining feedback from individual students can be used. There will be organisational and module evaluations that are occurring which should be taken into consideration when arranging any programme-wide feedback in order to avoid questionnaire fatigue. There will be times when you require targeted feedback on a particular aspect of the programme. Below are methods for collecting and analysing data from which the findings can be used to improve the quality of a programme to suit the needs of the student body.

Questionnaires

Questionnaires are commonly employed as a quality process for gathering the students' voices. These may be institutional requirements such as mid and end of module questionnaires. Whole cohort questionnaires can be a valuable source of information; these can be paper-based or more commonly today be via an electronic platform. Questionnaire design is a skill, and it is worth consulting textbooks on designing effective questionnaires. When considering the questions asked you should be mindful of how you will be evaluating the questionnaire and what you will be doing with the results. Another thing to consider is the deployment of the questionnaire. Emailing out the questionnaire for students to complete asynchronously will reduce your response rate and be open to a biased response. Only students who are motivated to respond either out of a sense of obligation or because they have an issue that they want feedback on are likely to complete the questionnaire. Questionnaires could be deployed during a teaching session, either face-to-face or virtually. If using an electronic platform with an instant collation of responses, you could display the anonymous responses and use this as a platform for discussion about the aspects you are evaluating. Quantitative data will show what people think but not necessarily why they are thinking that. Qualitative data will provide more depth of information. However, this takes longer to evaluate, and the approach taken will need to consider the size of the cohort.

SWOB analysis

SWOB (or SWOT) analysis is commonly used to reflect on personal strengths, weaknesses, opportunities, and barriers (or threats). A simple SWOB analysis is a powerful tool that can be used as an efficient way of providing rich feedback at programme level. It is a tool that can be used to structure feedback from students which can provide valuable information for planning the programme delivery (Romero-Gutierrez et al., 2016). It is used to generate ideas, not offer solutions (Leiber et al., 2018). For the purpose of programme evaluation each aspect can be viewed as follows:

Strengths – things that the students perceive are working well.
Weaknesses – things that students consider need to be improved.
Opportunities – things that students would like to see happen on the programme.
Barriers – things that get in the way of a student's study.

Application of a SWOB analysis

The self-analysis questionnaire can be distributed either as a paper-based exercise or electronically as necessary in a distance learning programme (Bornman, 2004). Here are two examples of how a SWOB analysis can be executed.

Face to face in a classroom setting:

Step one: decide on what aspect you are evaluating.
Step two: each student is provided with a piece of paper divided into four sections. Focusing on the chosen aspect they are asked to write what they perceive as strengths, weaknesses, opportunities, and barriers in each separate section.
Step three: the sheets are collected and reviewed. Depending on the number of participants, some of the issues raised can be openly discussed in the classroom. You may be able to provide an immediate response to some of the points made.
Step four: thank students for their contribution and let them know what you will do with the information.
Step five: collate the results and feedback to the students in a 'you said – we did' format.

In a virtual setting:

Step one: decide on what aspect you are evaluating.
Step two: record the session.
Step three: go through each section in turn giving students time to document their responses in the chat function. Acknowledge some responses as they appear, e.g. 'good point'. Allow sufficient time before moving on to the next section, i.e. wait for the comments in the chat to 'dry up'. Slides are useful to keep students focused on one aspect at a time, e.g. strengths, weaknesses, opportunities, and barriers.
Step four: thank the students for their responses and let them know what will happen to the data, i.e. when they can expect feedback on their comments.
Step five: using the recording of the session, collate and analyse the comments.
Step six: give feedback to the students in a 'you said–we did' format.

Student-led projects

Students can be a valuable asset when it comes to evaluating aspects of a programme. These may be done as part of a dissertation or as an extra-curricular activity. There is considerable benefit to students leading a project in that it reduces any hierarchy, leading to potentially more honest feedback. Students will pick areas to evaluate that are important to them, but there may be times when you can guide a student to a particular topic you would like to explore. Students are likely to need support in running their project, but running a project like this it will help them develop graduate skills.

Critical incident technique

The critical incident technique, developed by Flanagan (1954), is a way of collecting accounts of direct observation and perceptions. It can be used to gain information about factors that lead to satisfaction or dissatisfaction, usually in a targeted area. It helps to highlight areas of good and poor practice and in doing so identifies areas that impact on satisfaction with the programme. By focusing on specific experiences or issues and asking students to describe atypical experiences, both positive and negative, you can get in-depth understanding of their perceptions and feelings about the 'incidents'. Using this method also helps students focus on the positive aspects of the programme rather than just the negative.

The critical incident technique has been used over the years to capture the voice of the student. It is quicker and easier to design than a traditional questionnaire but will take longer to analyse than more structured questions (Jacques et al., 2009). Examples of its use include exploring effective teaching, learning, and assessment (Victoroff and Hogan, 2006; Douglas et al., 2008); students use of library facilities (Andrews, 1991); learning management systems (Islam, 2014); and student satisfaction (Douglas et al., 2015).

Critical incident technique is described as a flexible set of principles rather than a rigid technique (Butterfield et al., 2005). Using these following steps, you can adopt this overarching technique to collect data in a variety of methods including paper-based or electronic questionnaires, interviews, or focus groups.

- Step one is to decide on the area you wish to investigate
- Step two is to consider the most appropriate form of data collection. This will be determined by cohort size and area of practice, but a simple anonymous questionnaire can unveil more personal thoughts and feelings which a student may not want to reveal face to face.
- Step three is to ensure the students understand that you would like them to think about and describe an event or behaviour, something that impacted positively or negatively on an outcome. You are not looking for generic feedback.
- Step four is analysing the data. Using the information collected you should be able to identify themes or categories which relate to the area under investigation. This can be undertaken manually or using data analysis software.
- Step five is interpreting the findings and presenting the outcomes. You should have been able to identify a list of factors that impact on the phenomenon under investigation.

Vignette
Critical incident technique was used by one programme leader as part of a quality process to gather feedback on student placement experience. This was important as student placement constituted about 50 per cent of the programme. This was a paper-based activity undertaken in the classroom setting with 29 students. After an initial discussion about the activity, students were requested to document what makes a good day on placement and what makes a bad day on placement. These anonymous responses were collected, and the class was divided in half, with one group analysing the responses to what makes a good day and the other group analysing what makes a bad day. The process of putting the text into themes provided a platform for discussion about the issues raised. Students shared their experiences and offered solutions that they found worked for some of the issues. The opportunity to discuss their experiences for some students appeared to be a cathartic exercise. At the end of the session, the resultant themes were discussed and agreed upon. Information gleaned from the session was shared with placement providers and published (Naylor, 2019). This reinforces that the students' feedback is valued and acted upon.

Quality improvement

The financial and political pressures on higher education mean that quality improvement will be part of your role. There will be aspects of your programme that you want to change or there maybe external pressure to make changes to your programme. Whatever the driver, there are several tools and techniques that can be used and information about some of these has been provided below.

Lean Six Sigma

Universities across the world are starting to integrate Lean and Six Sigma for quality improvement. Six Sigma is a set of principles for improving processes that are said to increase reliability and reduce variation. These are tools and techniques are taken from industry and can be applied to a service sector such as higher education. As with many other service improvement strategies, it is a cyclical process of define, measure, analyse, improve, and control.

Six Sigma is often merged with lean principles aiming to streamline services and eliminate waste. It is a way of uncovering root causes and gain a better understanding of processes. Lean and Six Sigma are not without criticism. One is the lack of consideration for human factors, which are prominent in any service sector including higher education. It is customer-focused, which is important in this era of marketisation of higher education.

The Plan, Do, Study, Act (PDSA) model of quality improvement

The PDSA cycle is a framework that can be used to test out on a small scale any initiative that you would like to introduce. Using this model for improvement enables you to see if the proposed changes will work or if they need modifying. You can test out the impact of any changes in a way that is less disruptive than whole-scale implementation. It allows you to explore an idea with minimal risk of negative feedback or expense. This cycle has four stages as follows:

Plan: the stage in which you decide what changes you are going to make and how you are going to do this. You also need to decide what you are aiming for and how it will be evaluated.
Do: the stage in which you carry out the change on a small scale.
Study: based on predetermined measurable outcomes, and data you have collected before and after the introduction of a change, you study and reflect on the impact of the change.
Act: based on the information you have gathered and analysed you plan the next cycle or implementation of the initiative.

Using this model, as well as being able to test out the proposed changes, enables you to have evidence demonstrating the impact of the change. Looking at how people react to change differently in relation to engagement you would get a bell-shaped curve. A small number of early and enthusiastic adopters of the change, followed by the majority engaging with the change, leaving a small number of people who are later engagers. For this last group of people having evidence that the change is having a positive effect, particularly on students, helps them engage with the change. To help you succeed in introducing any change it is best to involve the early enthusiastic adopters at the start of the project.

Vignette
Following a low score on the NSS section on feedback, the PDSA cycle was used to introduce audio feedback into a programme in order to improve this area of academic practice.

Plan
During the planning stage representative stakeholders were identified and consulted about the idea. Feedback and experiences from both students and academics who had previous experience of audio feedback was obtained. Teams within the university for learning enhancement and technology were also approached for advice and guidance. Before starting, we established what we were trying to accomplish and why, i.e. aiming to improve the NSS score for assessment and feedback. We then needed to think about whom to involve in the project. This was to start on a small scale using one cohort and for a single assessment. If it had been a larger cohort, we might have considered asking for a small number of volunteers to trial the initiative. We also planned how to evaluate whether the initiative was successful or not.

Do
This is a stage in which the improvement was carried out. Testing the introduction of audio feedback with academics who believe that this will work rather than trying to convert people at this early stage. We introduced a small defined number of students in a set timescale. It was during this stage that we also gathered the information needed to evaluate the project. With this type of project, qualitative data in the form of focus groups was most appropriate.

Study
This is the stage where we paused and reflected on the project and the data gathered as part of the evaluation.

Act
This is the part where we planned for the next cycle. We made slight modifications and tested it out such as using a different platform for the audio feedback. The next PDSA cycle would be to try it on a slightly larger scale with a different set of students. We also needed to consider the sustainability of the initiative if it is no longer part of a project. How would we maintain enthusiasm for the use of audio feedback?

This is a cyclical process, and you can have as many iterations as required. You can also have simultaneous PDSA cycles that feed into one another.

Appreciative inquiry

Appreciative inquiry has a foundation in social constructivist philosophy. It is a way of thinking, shifting from problem-solving to a strengths-based approach to organisational development and quality improvement. Rather

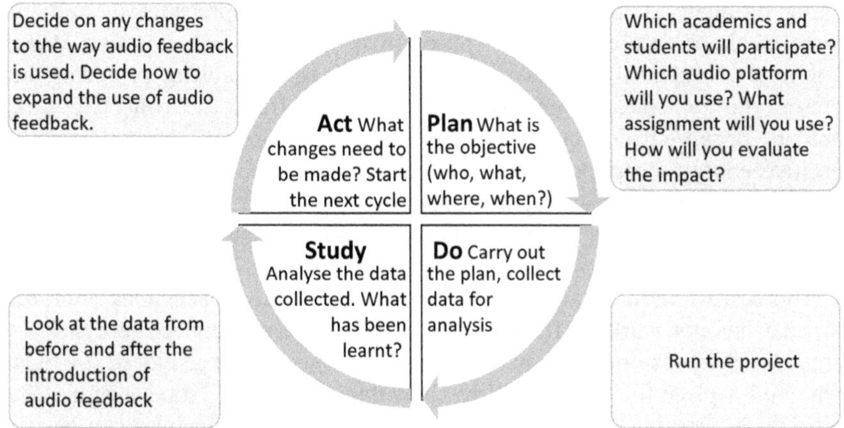

Figure 3.1 An example of the PDSA cycle

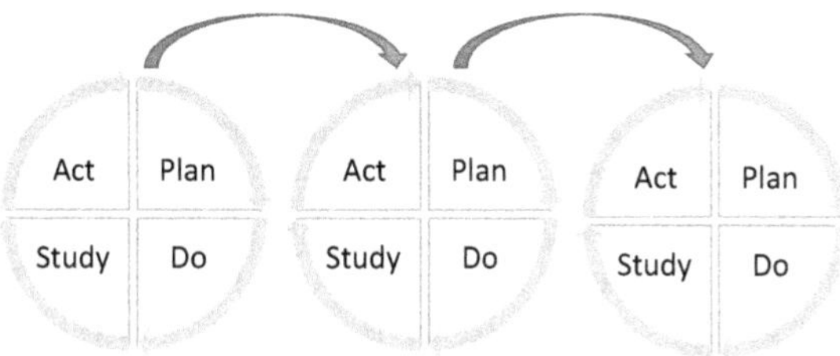

Figure 3.2 An example of a continuous PDSA cycle

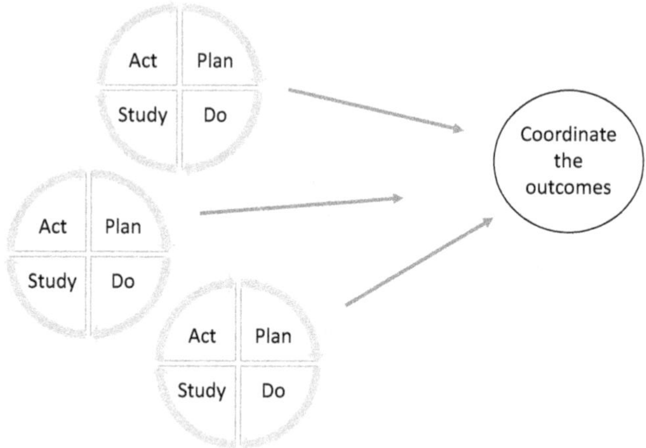

Figure 3.3 Simultaneous PDSA cycles

than looking at the negative aspects or poor feedback, one seeks to identify positive elements of the programme on which to build. Instead of focusing on fixing problems it identifies what is working well, appreciates it, and uses these to shape future practice. Appreciative inquiry is collaborative: it does not rely on external experts reviewing practices, diagnosing problems, and prescribing remedies; it involves change driven from the collective stakeholders. Because it does not look at problems or apportion blame it generates positive energy. People are more confident and comfortable with any developments because they are built on something familiar that has gone well in the past. In this way, appreciative inquiry is said to enhance self-esteem and self-expression (Whitney and Trosten-Bloom, 2010).

Appreciative inquiry takes careful facilitation because discussions often turn to what has not worked. Traditionally people will have received feedback and immediately focus on the poor results and what needs fixing. Indeed, there is a time and a place for fixing problems, but this tends to be reactive rather than proactively working on quality improvement. A set of principles can be used which form the 5D framework: Define, Discover, Dream, Design, Destiny.

Define: This first phase is where the topic is chosen to provide the focus for the remaining 4Ds. Ideally, the topic selection is by group consensus so that people take ownership of the following process. It should be something that you want to see grow and flourish, it should be positive. There should be genuine curiosity to explore the topic and there should be some purpose to it.
Discover: Through an inquiring discussion this stage seeks to understand the 'best of what is and what has been'. This can be done through one-to-one interviews, focus groups, or as part of a meeting. Conversations should be purposefully affirmative, sharing stories that are rich in description, drawing on the collective wisdom of those involved.

Dream: This phase is an exploration of 'what might be'. Usually undertaken in a group forum, it is the time for people to explore hopes and dreams for their work, module, and the programme. There should be an emphasis on being bold, looking beyond the restraints in the past.

Destiny: This step is where it is decided 'what will it be'. Through collaborative discussion steps to be taken going forwards, are decided upon, providing a framework for quality improvement. Once decided by the collective, the actual initiatives may be undertaken by small group working parties.

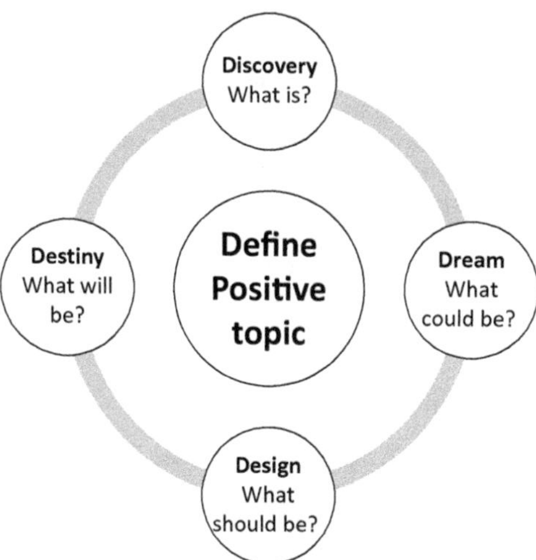

Figure 3.4 The appreciative inquiry cycle

Vignette

Appreciative inquiry was used by the programme leader of a taught doctoral programme. There was high attrition from the programme, especially from students who were academic members of staff at the institution. Rather than taking a problem-based approach, they used appreciative inquiry to explore the issue.

They first **defined** the topic as investigating factors that enabled a student to thrive on the programme.

Following this, a series of focus groups were held with students who had remained on the programme. During the focus groups, students relayed stories about what aspects of the programme were having a positive impact on their learning. From this, they **discovered** impacting factors of time and mentorship.

Students were also invited to the following phase of the process, that of exploring 'what might be'. This **dream** phase identified the desire for an increased amount of study time to be included in an academic workload and for identification of people willing to be mentors to academic staff undertaking a doctorate, in the initial stages of the programme in addition to the regular supervision during the research phase.

The **destiny** aspect of the process involved the programme delivery team working in consultation with senior managers to try and put these in place.

Reflection

The results of the National Student Survey have been published. You note with disappointment the scores for organisation and management, usually quite low, are even worse this year. You suspect the top-down interventions introduced the preceding year have not been successful and decide to take an appreciative inquiry approach. How would you do this?

The first thing to do is to narrow down the topic and have a clearly **defined** aspect to investigate; for example, the timetable.

Next you need to seek to understand the issues. Consider how you would gather this information, whom you would need to involve in the process? This should be students, but you may also consider involving year tutors and administrators responsible for timetabling. Think about how you will gather the information: will this be via a series of homogeneous interviews or focus groups, or by gathering all stakeholders together for one meeting to **discover** the issues?

Next is to **dream** of 'what might be'. Looking past any barriers to the ideal situation. During the discussion, if people start blocking the ideas as they are being aired you should try to facilitate a positive discussion, asking at this stage for participants to park any negative thoughts.

Once ideas have been generated the discussion should move on to identify any initiatives to be taken forward. At this point, you may generate an action plan and decide who will implement the initiatives, and how: the **destiny**.

Participatory action research

Participatory action research is commonly used in education. It is a collaborative process, engaging participants and ensuring that their voices can be heard. With this approach there is shared ownership; it is usually community-based and is orientated towards action. It has a cyclical and collaborative approach used to address a specific issue and is strongly influenced by reflective practice. In being cyclical there is potential for continuous refinement of any actions taken. It is a prolonged process, not a quick fix. Data is collected which initiates some action which is then reflected on. It is an iterative process. A typical cycle will include planning, action, reflection, evaluation. With

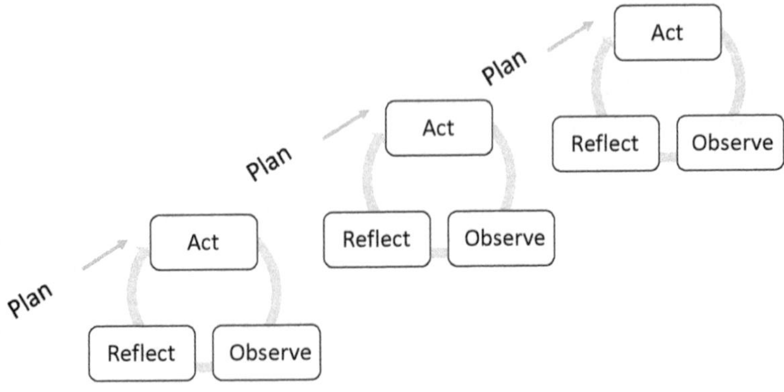

Figure 3.5 The participatory action research cycle

participator action research power is deliberately shared between the research and the researched, with those being researched empowered to become the researchers. When planning a project, you also need to consider representation. Is everybody who will be impacted by the outcomes of the research be represented on the project team? Any benefits coming out of the research have a direct benefit to those being researched.

Vignette

Participatory action research (PAR) was used within one programme to aid the development of technical skills by introducing peer-assisted learning. The initial cycle of PAR started with an invitation to third-year students to participate in the project. The first round of data collection was a focus group to gauge the views of the students about their own experiences and how they could use their experience to act as peer tutors to first-year students. The discussion was also around how they could facilitate the development of the technical skills, leading to the students discussing where when, and how to best engage with the peer-assisted learning with first-year students.

The next stage was action in which during a three-week period peer-assisted learning was undertaken. Following this a further focus group was held with the third years to explore the experiences of the participants. For this project, only one cycle of participatory action research was undertaken. Following the second focus group delivery of the peer-assisted learning could be refined, actioned, and reflected on. Due to time restraints and logistical arrangements first-year students were not active participants in this project. On reflection, this should have been considered to have a true representation of the people who would be impacted by the project. The primary researcher in this study was a member of the academic team. Students were involved in the design and delivery of the action and reflection but not analysis of the data. Further involvement in the project could have been facilitated with their participation in the analysis of the data from the focus groups and moving forward for students to organise and run the focus groups themselves.

Reflection

Consider an area of your programme that you would like to improve or build upon using participatory action research. With PAR there is a strong emphasis on collaboration. Therefore, you need to consider who will be involved in the project, what roles will they have, what expertise you need to bring in, how you will work together and who will facilitate the project? When planning you need to consider the following:

- What will be done?
- Who will be involved?
- Where would it take place?
- When will each stage take place?
- How will it be done?

Summary

As a programme leader, you will have some accountability for the quality of your programme. The move to students being viewed as customers introduces a competitive nature between institutions and you will be accountable for the quality of your programme. This chapter started by providing an overview of the changes in higher education and drivers behind quality assurance leading to the UK Quality Code for Higher Education and the teaching excellence and student outcomes framework. The expectations around quality assurance has been discussed with the rationale and practical tips for each aspect including external expertise, and engaging with the student body. Because quality assurance may require you to organise and chair meetings this has been divided into the different stages involved and practical advice provided on how to do them. Feedback plays an important part of quality assurance. There are several different ways to gather this evidence. This chapter introduces some strategies that work well for a programme leader. The financial and political pressures on higher education mean that quality improvement will be part of your role. Therefore, this chapter has included information about different collaborative approaches that can and have been used by programme leaders.

References

Advanced HE, 2019. Fundamentals of external examining. Available from https://s3.eu-west-2.amazonaws.com/assets.creode.advancehe-document-manager/documents/hea/Fundamentals%20of%20External%20Examining%20AHE%20-%20%20Feb%202019%20v2_1581086172.pdf.

Andrews, J., 1991. An exploration of students' library use problems. *Library Review,* 40(1). doi:10.1108/00242539110143096.

Bornman, G.M., 2004. Programme review guidelines for quality assurance in higher education. *International Journal of Sustainability in Higher Education*, 5(4), pp. 372–383. doi:10.1108/14676370410561072.

Butterfield, L.D., Borgen, W.A., Amundson, N.E., and Maglio, A.S.T., 2005. Fifty years of the critical incident technique: 1954–2004 and beyond. Qualitative Research, 5(4), pp. 475–497.

Dearing, R., 1997. The Dearing Report: Higher Education in the Learning Society. Available from http://www.educationengland.org.uk/documents/dearing1997/dearing1997.html.

Discover Uni (2021) Thinking about your uni choices? Available from https://discoveruni.gov.uk/ (accessed 15 October 2021).

Douglas, J., McClelland, R., and Davies, J., 2008. The development of a conceptual model of student satisfaction with their experience in higher education. *Quality Assurance in Education*, 13(4), pp. 263–276. doi:10.1108/09684880510700608.

Douglas, J.A., McClelland, R., Davies, J., and Sudbury, L., 2009. Using critical incident technique (CIT) to capture the voice of the student. The TQM Journal, 21(*4*), pp. 305–318. doi:10.1108/17542730910965038.

Douglas, J.A., Douglas, A., McClelland, R.J., and Davies, J., 2015. Understanding student satisfaction and dissatisfaction: An interpretive study in the UK higher education context. *Studies in Higher Education*, 40(2), pp. 329–349.

Flanagan, J.C., 1954. The critical incident technique. *Psychological Bulletin*, 51(4), pp. 327–358.

Harvey, L., 2005. A history and critique of quality evaluation in the UK. *Quality Assurance in Education*, 13(4), pp. 263–276. doi:10.1108/09684880510700608.

Her Majesty's Stationery Office, 1987. White Paper: Higher education: meeting the challenge. Available from http://www.educationengland.org.uk/documents/wp1987/1987-higher-ed.html#03.

Islam, A.N., 2014. Sources of satisfaction and dissatisfaction with a learning management system in post-adoption stage: A critical incident technique approach. *Computers in Human Behavior*, 30, pp. 249–261.

Jarratt, A., 1985. Report of the Steering Committee for Efficiency Studies in Universities, (The Jarratt Report). Retrieved from CVCP London.

Leiber, T., Stensaker, B. and Harvey, L.C., 2018. Bridging theory and practice of impact evaluation of quality management in higher education institutions: A SWOT analysis. *European Journal of Higher Education*, 8(3), pp. 351–365.

Naylor, S., 2019. Right place, right now: What makes a good day on placement? *Imaging and Therapy Practice*, December, pp. 13–18.

Office for Students, 2020. Quality and standards. Available from https://www.officeforstudents.org.uk/advice-and-guidance/regulation/quality-and-standards/quality-assessment-and-monitoring/.

Office for Students, 2021a. About the TEF. Available from https://www.officeforstudents.org.uk/advice-and-guidance/teaching/about-the-tef/ (accessed 15 October 2021).

Office for Students, 2021b. National Student Survey. Available from https://www.officeforstudents.org.uk/advice-and-guidance/student-information-and-data/national-student-survey-nss/nss-data-provider-level/ (accessed 15 October 2021).

Quality Assurance Agency, 2018. The right to award UK degrees. Available from https://www.qaa.ac.uk/docs/qaa/guidance/the-right-to-award-degrees-18.pdf?sfvrsn=4a2f781_14.

Quality Assurance Agency, 2018. United Kingdom Quality Code for Higher Education. Available from https://www.qaa.ac.uk/quality-code.

Quality Assurance Agency, 2019. Quality and Standards Review for Providers Registered with the Office for Students: Guidance for Providers. Available from https://www.qaa.ac.uk/en/reviewing-higher-education/types-of-review/quality-and-standards-review/providers-registered-with-the-ofs.

Romero-Gutierrez, M., Jimenez-Liso, M.R. and Martinez-Chico, M., 2016. SWOT analysis to evaluate the programme of a joint online/onsite master's degree in environmental education through the students' perceptions. *Evaluation and Program Planning*, 54, pp. 41–49.

United Kingdom Government, 1988. Education Reform Act 1988. Available from https://www.legislation.gov.uk/ukpga/1988/40/contents.

United Kingdom Government, 1990. Education (Student Loans) Act 1990. Available from https://www.legislation.gov.uk/ukpga/1990/6/enacted?view=extent&timeline=false.

United Kingdom Government, 1992. Further and Higher Education Act 1992. Available from https://www.legislation.gov.uk/ukpga/1992/13/contents.

United Kingdom Government, 2017. The Higher Education and Research Act 2017. Available from https://www.legislation.gov.uk/ukpga/2017/29/contents.

United Kingdom Standing Committee for Quality Assessment, 2020. Available from https://ukscqa.org.uk/.

Victoroff, K.Z. and Hogan, S. (2006). Students' perceptions of effective learning experiences in dental school: A qualitative study using a critical incident technique. *Journal of Dental Education*, 70(2), pp. 124–132.

Whitney, D.D. and Trosten-Bloom, A. (2010). *The power of appreciative inquiry: A practical guide to positive change.* Berrett-Koehler Publishers.

4 Programme design and approval

Programme validation and approval

Programmes go through a validation process during which the university establishes that a new programme is academically viable and that academic standards have been met. This is a quality process for which you will find guidelines, timescales, and hopefully advice from your institution. Revalidation is sometimes required whereby a programme is revisited during a formal event to ensure it continues to be fit for purpose. Revalidation is not always necessary as universities may operate an ongoing periodic review process. Revalidation may, however, be required where there is professional statutory or regulatory body (PSRB) accreditation or significant changes are being made to a programme. (Re)validation and PSRB (re)approval often go hand in hand with joint events. Validation events are very structured, during which you will present your programme to a panel of people from within the university, external representatives, and representatives from your PRSB if applicable. The panel may meet with industry partners, students and service users if appropriate to your programme. The panel has a chair whose role is to facilitate the event and ensure that judgement about your programme is fair. The panel discusses the programme leading to various outcomes including recommendations, commendations, and conditions for approval. A report is produced after the event to which you will be required to respond.

As programme leader your role in this process may include:

- leading the programme team in preparation for validation;
- collating the production of relevant documentation;
- briefing colleagues before the validation event;
- consulting with relevant professional services departments;
- nominating a suitable external panel member;
- liaising with the PRSB;
- devising and maintaining appropriate timescales;
- ensuring appropriate levels of consultation have been used to inform the development of the programme;
- presenting information about the programme to the validation panel;

DOI: 10.4324/9781003126355-5

- after the validation, preparing responses to any conditions and/or recommendations made at the validation.

This can be a daunting process so here are some ideas that may be helpful.

Top tips for programme validation and approval

1 Start the process as early as possible. There will be many stages to go through, usually starting with approval from a university committee who will assess if there is a market for the programme.
2 Contact the quality department within your university and access any guidance and training provided.
3 It is useful to contact other academics who have recently undertaken this process for advice and guidance.
4 Consultation about the programme should be wide-reaching, comprehensive, robust, and well documented. Below is a list suggesting whom to include:

   a students;
   b alumni;
   c service users;
   d employers;
   e placement providers;
   f teaching and learning team;
   g marketing team;
   h strategic planning;
   i library services;
   j timetabling services;
   k admissions;
   l careers and employability services.

5 Ensure you have mapped to internal and external benchmarks; for example, the university's learning and teaching strategy and professional and regulatory body requirements.
6 Work within your university's strategies; for example, learning and teaching strategy
7 Consider the resources required to deliver the programme including placements.
8 Engage with a critical friend who can sense check your documents.
9 Ensure your documentation has been thoroughly proofread.
10 The documents are large and version control is essential, particularly with a collaborative approach to document writing.
11 Set aside time in your diary for writing the documents and the report following the validation event.
12 Identify some support for you such as a buddy, mentor, or line manager who can support you through the process.

Further advice and guidance can be found from the QAA (2018).

Stakeholders

When designing your programme, it is important to identify all your stakeholders. The National Health Institute for Innovation and Improvement (2008) produced a 9Cs checklist to help identify stakeholders. You can use this to produce a map of your own stakeholders.

1 commissioners: those who pay towards the programme;
2 customers: those who access the programme, i.e. students, alumni;
3 collaborators: those with whom the organisation works to deliver the programme, i.e. library services;
4 contributors: those who provide content for the programme, i.e. module leaders;
5 channels: people and organisations who provide the programme with a route to a customer;
6 commentators: those whose opinions of the programme are heard by customers and others;
7 consumers: those who are served by our graduates; i.e. patients, the community, users;
8 champions: those who believe in and will actively promote the programme;
9 competitors: those working in the same area who offer a similar programme.

With a student-centred approach, one of the most important stakeholders is your student. With this in mind, you could consider co-creation of your curriculum.

Co-creation of the curriculum

Students co-creating the curriculum is not a new concept but has gained in popularity over recent years. This student-centred approach challenges thinking around programme design and promotes active engagement between students and staff. It empowers students, developing a sense of shared ownership and responsibility for the teaching and learning process (Lubicz-Nawrocka, 2018). It is a shift in ethos from students having a passive role in their education to being partners in their learning (Taylor and Bovill, 2018). Bovill and Woolmer (2019) identify the difference between co-creation *in* and co-creation *of* the curriculum. In this chapter co-creation of the curriculum will be discussed. Other aspects of co-creation were discussed in Chapter 3 in relation to the quality of your programme.

The concept of co-creating the curriculum is not widespread but can be found in pockets within institutions. It is a practice that challenges traditional institutional structures and established power dynamics. Different terminology is used such as students as partners, as change agents, or as producers (Bovill, 2019). A familiar term within the UK is 'student engagement'. This covers a range of activities from students engaging with their learning materials to students as partners (Bovill, 2020). Another commonly used phrase is student 'voice', often associated with gaining student feedback (Cook-Sather, 2020).

The student's role as co-creator can come in a variety of forms. Variables include the number of students involved and the extent of their involvement. These can range from a small number of selected student representatives, consultation with past students, or involvement of whole cohorts (Lubicz-Nawrocka, 2018; Bovill, 2020). Co-creation could be the complete development or redesign of a programme, co-development of resources, or for part of a programme, for example co-designing of assessment strategies. Students may be part of a curriculum design committee, working alongside academics at the start of the process, through to curriculum approval. Bovill (2019) has created a co-creation of learning and teaching typology as a tool to support students and staff plan co-creation. It asks a series of questions that will help articulate the intentions of your co-creation:

- Who initiates the co-creation?
- What is the focus of the co-creation?
- What is the context for co-creation?
- Have you selected your students from a larger group or involved the whole class?
- Which students are involved?
- What is the scale of the co-creation?
- How long does the co-creation last?
- What is the role of the student?
- What is the nature of the student involvement?
- What is the nature of the reward or recompense given to the student?
- Why are you co-creating?

The benefits of co-creation have been identified as shared responsibility, respect, and trust (Lubicz-Nawrocka, 2018). The creation of a strong collaborative learning community can have a transformative effect for both students and staff. From an academic point of view, co-creation can have a positive impact on job satisfaction. These benefits can only materialise if co-creation is embraced holistically, not tokenistic. Not only listening to students but genuinely valuing their contribution. This will only happen if staff and students understand the benefits (Murphy et al., 2017). Through an experimental design study, measuring students' academic achievement Doyle et al. (2021) found that co-creation had a positive impact on student performance

Co-creation is democratic, engaging, and inclusive; it can help to internationalise the curricula by recognising students' perspectives from the diverse student body (Lubicz-Nawrocka, 2018; Wijaya Mulya, 2019). This democratic approach and shared decision-making encourages students to value the opinions of others and consider the needs of other students (Wijaya Mulya, 2019). It can build reciprocal respect for the staff and student voices, as well as develop self-respect (Cook-Sather, 2020). It can help to develop more equitable teaching and learning experiences for students and provide a meaningful and authentic relationship between students and academics (Lubicz-Nawrocka, 2018). A student participating in the study by Lubicz-Nawrocka (2018) describes their involvement as being beneficial in the development of transferable skills.

Co-creation comes with both philosophical and practical difficulties (Murphy et al., 2017). Bovill (2019) describes a whole-class approach to co-creation, identifying challenges around the time constraints, class size, and challenging cohorts. There is resistance to creation as it can be seen as risky and time-consuming (Lubicz-Nawrocka, 2018; Bovill and Woolmer, 2019). A staff member who participated in the mixed-methods study by Murphy et al. (2017) voiced concerns of being wary about giving too much power to students but felt quite happy responding to their feedback. There were also concerns about students lacking expertise and subject knowledge enough to contribute to a true partnership. Some academics are concerned that being flexible to the desires of the students in terms of their learning and development may be at odds with the requirements of the labour market (Wijaya Mulya, 2019). Co-creation of the curriculum changes the relationship between student and teacher thus changing the status quo of traditional power dynamics (Lubicz-Nawrocka, 2018). Thus, a barrier is an academic's self-perception as the change in power may challenge their professional legitimacy (Murphy et al., 2017). Whilst the ideal is a shared partnership, it has been recognised that academic staff will normally take the lead in managing the process (Lubicz-Nawrocka, 2018). There is also a need to manage the perceptions of students who could view curriculum development as the responsibility of academic staff and by devolving this responsibility students are somehow shirking their responsibilities.

On balance, although co-creation can be challenging the benefits, particularly in ensuring the programme is internationalised and meets sustainable development goals, make it a valuable approach to consider.

Reflection

Using the questions below consider how you will involve students in the development of your curriculum:

- What approach will you use for the co-creation of your curriculum?
- How will you recruit students to be involved in your curriculum development?
- How will you ensure students have an equal voice in the process?

Industry involvement in curriculum development

Placement providers, employers, and people using their services all need to be involved in the development of a programme to ensure it is fit for its purpose. Service-user involvement in all aspects of healthcare has been on the agenda for well over a decade. It is incorporated into the standards of education and training for both the Health and Care Professions Council (2018) and the Nursing and Midwifery Council (2018). However, for all programmes it is important to consider the consumers, and people who will benefit from the students' education. There are excellent examples of co-production. Some models involve a partnership in which employers, service users, and academic staff contribute to the programme design, resulting in the potential to embed consumer perspectives into the core of programmes. However, some approaches risk the dilution or compromise consumer perspectives, or may end up being a marginal and tokenistic involvement.

Service-user events or symposiums can be used to help develop the involvement of service users in a programme as seen by Carter and Brown (2014) who moved from just adult service users to incorporating children and young people into the development of a child nurse curriculum. They sought the views of children via interviews and a survey. So, although they did not form part of the curriculum development team, their voice in the curriculum development process was heard. Another way of accessing service users, particularly used in mental health, is via involvement centres. In their research, El Enany et al. (2013) used an involvement centre set up and run by one NHS trust. These service-user organisations have 'experts by experience' who have often had the training to help fulfil the role of consultant. Also, in the field of mental health, the process used by Masters et al. (2002) involved a joint project working between academic team members, mental health students, mental health service users, and carers. User and carer representatives for the project were recruited via user and carer-led organisations such as involvement groups and forums. Although not without issues, the project involved having active inclusion of service users on the strategic development group.

The consumer can have an impact on the programme along a continuum from consultation to collaboration and co-production.

Change management

The reapproval and revalidation of your programme provide an opportunity to pause and reflect, allowing changes to the programme. Change management can be challenging, and tools such as the PDSA cycle can help. More strategies for quality improvement were covered in Chapter 3. You should also consider the best leadership approach from those discussed in Chapter 1. A collective style of leadership will help the programme delivery team feel more engaged with and take ownership of developing a new programme. A major consideration for your programme will be the curriculum.

Curriculum justification

The curriculum represents the planned learning experience of the students. It has four main aspects: content, teaching and learning strategies, assessment, and evaluation. Today's curricular has moved from being teacher-dominated, focusing

Collaboration
Consultation
Having active inclusion of consumers on the strategic development group
Inviting representatives to join programme development meetings
Joint project working between academic team members, students, and consumers.
Holding a series of separate events to consult with consumers
Consultation via established consumer groups
Undertaking data collection via surveys or interviews with consumers
Accessing consumer opinion via social media such as relevant chat rooms

Figure 4.1 Levels of involvement

mainly on what the teacher will deliver, to student-centred, considering the whole student experience. Over the years there has been debate about the model of curriculum development. Some models are more concerned with the end product rather than the means of a curriculum (product models) whilst others focus on the student activities and experience (process models). It is generally now considered that learning objectives should describe what we want the student to learn and observable behaviours rather than the method of instruction. The classification of learning objectives most commonly used to assist in formulating objectives is that developed by Benjamin Bloom. The three domains of learning – cognitive, affective, and psychomotor – all require development. Planning and sequencing within the curriculum is essential to ensure that the students progress.

Many tools can be used to assist with planning the content of the curriculum. Curriculum maps, learning spirals, and concept maps all help in planning what we need the student to learn. One of the first stages in this planning is to look at the current situation and all the factors that need to be considered.

Situation analysis

A situation analysis is looking at the internal and external factors that impact and input into the development of your curricular. These will include institutional policies and strategies, national guidelines as well as professional and regulatory body requirements. Before starting to plan your curriculum, it is a worthwhile exercise to pause and gather information about all the impacting factors you need to consider, possibly using a table similar to Table 4.1.

Table 4.1 Situation analysis

Factor	*Influence on learning and teaching*	*Curriculum decision*
External influences e.g. Regulatory body Standards of Proficiency		
Internal influences e.g. HEI Teaching and Learning Strategy		
The learner e.g. Internationalising the curriculum		
The programme delivery team e.g. Placement capacity		

Techniques for consultation

It has been established that consultation with a variety of stakeholders is essential in developing an effective programme. This can be challenging due to the diversity of the stakeholders. The vignette and techniques below provide examples of techniques that can be used.

Vignette

As programme leader for a BSc Diagnostic Radiography, I was leading the revalidation of the programme. This is a fast-developing profession and there had been many changes both in technology and in ways of working. A thorough consultation with employers was required to ensure graduates from the programme were ready to join the profession. A large proportion of the programme was conducted at placement sites and around 80 per cent of graduates found employment at their placement site; therefore these were appropriate sources for gaining opinions on the skills that needed developing during the programme. Due to the widespread location and the acknowledgement that department managers are busy people I used a Delphi technique to obtain a consensus of what was required in the new programme.

A truly collaborative approach to programme development will bring together a variety of stakeholders. These people may have a different experience of being in and contributing to a discussion. Some may be more reticent in voicing their opinion than others. One technique I have used to overcome these issues is a nominal group technique. This structured format enables all participants in a meeting to have their opinion heard and discussed. Information about these two strategies can be found below.

Nominal group technique (NGT)

NGT is an organised, highly structured group activity designed to elicit the views of the participants on a given topic. It was initially designed as a method of group decision-making (Delbecq et al., 1975). The strategy generates ideas from participants individually, which can then be discussed in a controlled manner, and ranked by the members of the group. The stages of the process include a silent period during which individuals note down their ideas from a predefined question, a round robin collation of those ideas, a serial discussion to clarify the ideas, a vote on the items of importance followed by further discussion on the pattern of the voting and a final vote to rank the ideas according to their level of importance. Although some authors suggest that it provides quantitative as well as qualitative data, it does not give definitive results, only suggestive ones (Lloyd-Jones et al., 1999, Perry and Linsley, 2006). NGT meetings provide just a snapshot of group opinion, which may change over time (Gaskin, 2003).

There are many reported uses of NGT. These include: to obtain the views of stakeholders (Steward, 2001; Williams et al., 2006; Castiglioni et al., 2008), as a curriculum or course evaluation tool (Dobbie et al., 2004; Kiely, 2003; Lancaster et al., 2002; Lloyd-Jones et al., 1999; Perry and Linsley, 2006), and for developing guidelines and research priorities (Allen et al., 2004). Some have used it in the past as a qualitative research tool (Gallagher et al., 1993; Carney et al., 1996). Kidd and Parshall (2000) suggest that NGT is more suitable than a focus group when a consensus is a required outcome of the meeting, where the participants were required to agree on the issues most important to them as is the case with programme development.

There is much debate about the optimum number for a nominal group meeting. Delbecq et al. (1975) suggest between five and nine. Less than five people lack the resources to provide enough ideas to be able to analyse the problem and more than nine will not increase the accuracy of the group (Delbecq et al., 1975). De Ruyter (1996) undertook a comparative study on group size and found that the number of items generated increased as the group size increased, but that seven in the group produced the highest quality. This number also yielded the best results regarding participant satisfaction (De Ruyter, 1996). It is also possible that with smaller numbers the participants will feel more exposed and this could be mildly threatening to the participants (Carney et al., 1996). Others have suggested between seven and nine (Gaskin, 2003) and most authors have used these numbers (Lloyd-Jones et al., 1999; Steward, 2001) although some used slightly more (Perry and Linsley, 2006; Williams et al., 2006) and others from necessity, or choice, have used less (Carney et al., 1996; Lancaster et al., 2002).

The process

The trigger question

Preparation of the trigger question for an NGT meeting is essential to its success (Gaskin, 2003; Williams et al., 2006). It is important to pilot the question to ensure that it will produce ideas relevant to the aim of the meeting. More than one trigger question can be used (Dobbie et al., 2004; Lloyd-Jones et al., 1999; Perry and Linsley, 2006). Potentially the more questions used as a trigger the more ideas will be generated. This could extend the process and produce an unmanageable number of ideas (Dobbie et al., 2004; Lloyd-Jones et al., 1999; Perry and Linsley, 2006). The question should be designed to be unambiguous, focus on one topic, and use simple language (Carney et al., 1996; Gaskin, 2003). A poorly prepared question is more likely to elicit vague, muddled responses (Carney et al., 1996); whereas a well-prepared question can produce high-quality specific ideas (Van de Ven and Delbecq, 1974). The trigger question should be presented to the participants who then have five minutes of silence in which to note down any ideas that are generated by the question.

The round-robin phase

Once the ideas have been generated the round robin phase gives the participants a chance to put forward one idea in turn. If the participants run out of ideas you can allow them to miss a go. As the list progresses, participants may think of new issues; prompted by the contribution of another member of the group, they can join in and give these new ideas. This is called 'hitchhiking'. If another member of the group has already raised an issue it does not need duplicating unless deemed slightly different by the participant. The benefits of this stage are that each participant is given equal 'floor space' and the list of ideas is displayed before any discussion begins. According to Debecq et al. (1975) an average NGT meeting will generate over 12 items in each group. The participants in some meetings have produced between 12 and 40 items (Castigilioni et al., 2008; Williams et al., 2006).

Discussion of ideas

Step three of the process following the round-robin tabulation of ideas is a serial discussion and clarification of those ideas. This takes a non-threatening format where the person who generated the idea was not responsible for defending or clarifying that idea. The open discussion to clarify the ideas is undertaken amicably. However, if any judgemental comments or criticisms are made they should be quashed (Carney et al., 1996). It is the role of the facilitator to ensure the smooth running of the group, rather than lead the discussion (Carney et al., 1996). Time management is very important in this section to ensure that all the ideas received equal attention. The structure prevents digression from the topic. Following the serial discussion, by mutual agreement items can be combined into themes.

Initial ranking and discussion

Once all the items have been discussed, the participants are asked to individually pick the five that were most important to them and then rank them in order of importance. Once the pattern of the ranking had been displayed it is discussed and interpreted by the participants, with minimal facilitation.

Final vote

A final voting stage then takes place where participants can either keep to their original five issues and give them a level of importance on a scale of one to ten or can change their minds following the discussion. The final vote produces a list of items in order of importance and the results once again are discussed with the participants. This final stage produces a perceived sense of closure and a feeling of accomplishment (Van de Ven and Delbecq, 1974).

The Delphi technique

The Delphi method, similar to the nominal group technique, can be used to help develop your curriculum (Green, 2014; Coezer and Sitlington, 2014). It is used to gather and converge opinions, reaching a consensus without bringing individuals together. Delphi technique was introduced in the 1950s as a planning and decision-making tool (Gupta and Clarke 1996). Since then there have been various adaptations to the process (Hsu et al., 2019; Rajhans et al., 2020). The basic principles are a structured process of interspersed questionnaires and controlled feedback and all participants remain anonymous. It facilitates group decision-making and is a useful technique for instances where it is impractical due to time or location to bring people together. This was a useful technique to use during the pandemic where face-to-face contact was limited (Rajhans et al., 2020). This lack of direct contact with respondents can have the drawback of the lack of social integration reducing the motivation to respond (Green, 2014). When in a paper-based format relying on a postal service the whole process could be very time-consuming and labour-intensive. However, with modern technology making communication easier via email or other computer software Delphi technique is much more appealing. It is appropriate for curriculum development for all of the following reasons:

- Curriculum development benefits from the collective subjective opinions.
- Those whom we would want to contribute to the curriculum do not routinely meet together.
- A wide range of expertise may be sought without the dominant opinions of one group overpowering another.
- The number of people involved may be too great for meaningful conversation.
- Time and cost may put constraints around meeting face-to-face.

The Delphi technique process

The process starts by recruiting a panel of experts who are asked to provide their opinion on a specific topic such as what they consider should be included in the contents of your curriculum. Your panel of experts should be chosen based on whom you consider will have a valid opinion on your curriculum. The technique relies on gathering the opinions of a wide heterogeneous range of participants. It is a particularly useful technique for gathering opinions of students and alumni about the curriculum. Without the necessity to attend a face-to-face meeting it is also a convenient method of gathering opinions from experts from industries relevant to your programme. Experts should be recruited for the panel who have some enthusiasm for the process. This is a cyclical technique and you will want to keep the dropout rate to a minimum. Ideally, the people you select should have opinions that you want to elicit and an interest in the programme you are developing. You may wish to include representatives on your panel from current students, alumni, placement providers, representatives from your profession, and other people with specialist knowledge such as from the teaching and learning team within the institution. The broad range of participants is essential to avoid introducing bias into your curriculum plans. The size of the panel can vary tremendously; however, you do need to be pragmatic about how much data you wish to generate considering the time available. It is the quality of the responses that is more important than the number of items generated. The panel members remain anonymous, this has the advantage that anonymity encourages opinions that are less likely to be influenced, or persuaded by others. It is also particularly applicable if you want to gather the opinions of a wide range of experts where one group may be more dominant than another. However, the lack of anonymity may result in responses that are less considered because the expert does not need to be answerable to their responses.

It is usual to have three rounds within a Delphi technique. However, consensus may be reached after two rounds or you may need more than three rounds. You should bear in mind the timeframe and keep this as tight as possible to maintain interest in the curriculum development. For example, you may want to keep to a gap of only about two weeks between the distribution of the questionnaires. Good communication with the participants is important for a successful Delphi technique process.

Round one

The purpose of the first round is to form a list of items. This is unstructured using a trigger record question to seek open responses. The initial key question should be clear, concise, and unambiguous. The questionnaire must be pretested to ensure that it elicits the type of responses that you expect. A questionnaire should be distributed with a covering letter explaining the process.

Round two

The second round provides the experts' panel with a copy of the collective list of items generated from the first round in the form of a questionnaire. This list should be edited and collated to form a manageable list of items. It takes the format of a predetermined scale similar to a Likert scale and the experts are required to rate the items on the questionnaire. For example: very important – important – not important.

Round three

For the third round, the experts are provided with feedback on the previous round with the collated rankings of the items. Participants are asked to re-examine their opinions where they differ significantly from other experts on the panel. This final round will indicate where a consensus can be made and where it cannot be reached. By the end of the process, you should have a comprehensive list of items to consider when developing your curriculum. As well as meeting the requirements of the stakeholders, some broader themes need to be considered.

Major themes to consider within your curriculum

Education for sustainable development

Students are coming to university expecting sustainability to be incorporated into their education. The student-led charity Students Organising for Sustainability (2021) aims to bring about change through education. Seventeen sustainable development goals were adopted by the member states of the United Nations (UN) in 2015 (UN, 2021). The goals are detailed in the table below, the aim of which is to end extreme poverty, protect the planet, and ensure prosperity for all by 2030 (UN, 2021). There is a specific focus on education for sustainable development, aiming to ensure that learners acquired the knowledge and skills needed to promote sustainable development (Leicht et al., 2018). We must raise awareness of this amongst our students, increasing their sustainable development literacy. Advance HE and QAA have published guidance to help you incorporate education for sustainable development into your curricula (Advance HE and QAA, 2021).

At present, there is a lack of a consistent approach between higher education institutions as well as between programmes within any one university. Different perspectives and personal approaches result in considerable complexity around addressing the goals for sustainable development. A whole university approach is recommended, possibly using a 4C-model for embedding sustainability development; Campus, Curriculum, Community, Culture (Selby, 2009). Cultural changes are needed within universities to drive the sustainability agenda, but this is a slow process and enthusiastic individuals may find a lack of support from within their university (Ávila et al., 2017). Much of the work on raising awareness of sustainable development is driven by committed academics working in isolation (Leal Filho et al., 2018). As a programme leader, you should be considering embedding sustainability

Table 4.2 The sustainable development goals (UN, 2021)

Sustainable development goals	
No poverty	End poverty in all its forms everywhere
Zero hunger	End hunger, achieve food security and improved nutrition, and promote sustainable agriculture
Good health and well-being	Ensure healthy lives and promote well-being for all at all ages
Quality education	Ensure inclusive and equitable quality education and promote lifelong learning opportunities for all
Gender equality	Achieving gender equality and empowering all women and girls
Clean water and sanitation	Ensure availability and sustainable management of water and sanitisation for all
Affordable and clean energy	Ensure access to affordable reliable, sustainable, and modern energy for all
Decent work and economic growth	Promote sustained, inclusive, and sustainable economic growth, full and productive employment, and decent work for all
Industry, innovation, and infrastructure	Build resilient infrastructure, Promote inclusive and sustainable industrialization and foster innovation.
Reduce inequalities	Reduce income inequality within and among countries
Sustainable cities and communities	Make cities and human settlements inclusive, safe resilient and sustainable
Responsible consumption and production	Ensure sustainable consumption and production patterns
Climate action	Take urgent action to combat climate change and its impacts by regulating emissions and promoting developments in renewable energy
Life below water	Concern and sustainably use the oceans seas and marine resources for sustainable development
Life on land	Protect restore and promote sustainable use of terrestrial ecosystems, sustainably manage forests, combat desertification, and halt and reverse land degradation and halt biodiversity loss.
Peace, justice and strong institutions	Promote peaceful and inclusive societies for sustainable development, provide access to justice for all and build effective, accountable, inclusive institutions at all levels.
Partnerships for the goals	Strengthen the means of implementation and not revitalize the global partnership for sustainable development

Source: United Nations, 2021. The 17 Goals. Available from https://sdgs.un.org/goals

development within your curriculum. This will take motivation and recognition of the need for change (Leal Filho et al., 2018). To help, you may find communities of practice within your organisation that you can join, and

Advance HE has produced a sustainable development toolkit, a resource that can be used to introduce sustainable development into your programme (Kemp, 2015). Further guidance is available from the Future Fit Framework (Sterling, 2010).

UNESCO suggests key competencies for sustainability (UNESCO, 2021). Below are some areas for you to consider when planning your curriculum to help develop these:

1 Help students to become critical thinkers and consider their attitudes and values about global sustainable development by engaging students in deep debates on ethical issues.
2 Help students engage with their local community to gain a broad understanding of societal needs.
3 Expose students to authentic real-world situations and use case studies for them to critically analyse and contextualise theory.
4 Enrich the student experience through exposure to outside agencies, for example people from industry and service users.
5 Consider your development and that of other academics in relation to understanding sustainability goals.

Some strategies have been identified to support the development of sustainability literacy:

- **Transformative learning** using participatory pedagogy that promotes critical self-reflection helps students address complex multi-stakeholder real-life problems (Leal Filho et al., 2018).
- **A collaborative, interdisciplinary approach** is advisable to replicate real-world situations (Lozano et al., 2017; Leal Filho et al., 2018). Annan-Diab and Molinari (2017) describe their multi-professional initiative as a practical approach for encouraging students to engage with sustainable development and utilised this within management programmes. There are barriers to integration between disciplines which can be structural, organisational, or protectionist.
- **Role-playing scenarios** where students are required to apply their knowledge to a given problem and reflect on issues is one way of placing them in a real-world context and experience the complexity of decision-making (Annan-Diab and Molinari, 2017)
- **Work-based learning**, for example placing students in developing countries or within their community, gives them direct exposure to the complexity of real-world situations (Leal Filho et al., 2018).
- **Community outreach** programmes can have a transformative effect as students challenge their own stereotypes and personal values (Ávila et al., 2017).

Reflection

Looking at the information about sustainable development. Using the questions below as a prompt, consider how you will incorporate this into your programme.

- What training is available to you to develop your understanding of education for sustainable development?
- What opportunities can you provide for students to apply their learning in their community?
- What people from industry or service users can you identify who can become involved in your programme?
- How will you recognise extracurricular activities undertaken by students?

Internationalising the curricula

Internationalisation is becoming a prominent focus within higher education institutions around the world. The fifth global survey by the International Association of Universities on internationalisation found out more than 90 per cent have internationalisation in their mission statements or strategic plan (Marinoni, 2019). This focus on internationalisation is driven by a combination of political, economic, and societal change. These include the marketisation and massification of higher education, widening participation, and the need for students to develop global perspectives. There is criticism that these bold institutional statements are not being applied to teaching and learning (Green, 2019) and that a gap exists between theory and practice (Ryan et al., 2021).

The view of internationalisation in terms of just the mobility of students, with a focus on recruiting international students, is shifting, to have a stronger emphasis on internationalisation of the curriculum (Green, 2019). This is about incorporating international and intercultural dimensions into teaching, learning, and assessment (Leask, 2015). Internationalisation is contextual, with different disciplines interpreting it in different ways (Ryan et al., 2021). Studies looking at lecturers' engagement with internationalisation have found that whilst there is a willingness to engage in internationalisation, they do not fully understand the concept, and struggle to embed it into their module (Ryan et al., 2021). A case study published by the Higher Education Academy identified that some staff wrongly considered that they already take this on-board. There are pockets of good practice and they made staff development the central focus of the project (Cameron, 2018). To produce interculturally competent, socially responsible, globally aware students it may require academics to also reflect on their personal perspectives and intercultural competence (Green, 2019).

For initiatives to succeed students and staff must see the relevance of internationalisation (Jones, 2017). They also need to recognise the changing nature and demographics within student cohorts. Internationalisation can enhance the curricula by both making it more inclusive for students from diverse ethnic backgrounds and preparing all students for the multicultural world of work into which they will be entering (de Wit, 2019). It can lead to a more meaningful and inclusive student experience with relevant curricula which will improve graduate employability (Ryan et al., 2021).

Internationalising the curricula may require academics to consider their own discipline in terms of culture and the breadth of perspective included in its content. They may be unsure how to do this or lack confidence (Clifford, 2009; Green, 2019; Ryan et al., 2021). Some disciplines find this harder than others as changing deeply entrenched traditions can be difficult (Clifford, 2009). This difference in disciplines is also replicated in students' views on internationalisation (Heffernan et al., 2019). Ryan et al. (2021) suggest one way to develop academics is for them to engage in a community of practice, giving them space and time in which to reflect and explore different perspectives. An inclusive team approach to curriculum development will also be helpful (Clifford, 2009). A collaborative approach will be valuable, particularly for staff who have limited multicultural experience. Collaborating with international students, staff, and external practitioners will facilitate a broader perspective (Clifford, 2009). Staff and students from multicultural backgrounds can act as 'champions', being mentors and change agents (Cameron, 2018).

Making changes to the course content alone may fail to fully develop an internationalised curriculum. Changes to the pedagogy, considering the learning process and assessment should also be considered (Green, 2019). Leask (2015) suggests an action research approach to internationalising the curricula. Action research is discussed in relation to quality in Chapter 3. When designing a programme, alongside the formal curricula you should consider the extracurricular activity and what Jones (2017) identifies as the hidden curriculum, the development of personal values and beliefs. Leask (2015) provides a conceptual framework for internationalising a curriculum, prompting exploration from different perspectives. The first stage is to define internationalisation in terms of your discipline. To do this effectively you will need to engage with your discipline team (Fragouli, 2020). Start by looking at your current curricula and identifying how international it is now. This should be done from different stakeholders' perspectives. Then through discussion with colleagues, you can identify areas for development, and produce an action plan.

Enablers for success include:

- clarifying why and how the curriculum is internationalised;
- considering all students on the programme both international and home;
- involving people who can support the process;
- paying careful attention to learning outcomes;
- facilitating reflection about internationalisation with both staff and students;
- recognising that internationalising the curriculum is a complex, challenging process and that academic staff may require support.

(Jones, 2017)

When developing learning outcomes for an internationalised curricular you could include the following adapted from Jones and Killick, (2013) and Green and Mertova, (2016).

Aspects relating to global perspective:

knowledge of other countries and cultures;
Understanding the global economy and politics;
Developing a global outlook.

Intercultural competence:

demonstrating self-awareness in terms of own culture and perspectives;
reflecting on their own cultural identity;
demonstrating sensitivity to the perspective of others;
developing an empathetic approach;
developing communication skills;
demonstrating inclusive behaviour.

Becoming a responsible global citizen:

Developing a great awareness around issues of equality and social justice;
Reducing prejudice stereotyping and discrimination;
Recognising and understanding sustainability and ethical issues;
A positive reaction to change.

It may be possible to adapt your current learning outcomes. Jones and Killick, (2013) provide examples of how existing learning outcomes can be modified to be more in keeping with an internationalised curriculum, for example by adding words such as global, multicultural, and international.

Learning and teaching strategies for internationalising the curriculum include:

- forming international partnerships;
- making use of visiting practitioners and tapping into external expertise;
- ensuring literature and research from other countries are used in teaching;
- providing opportunities for intercultural interaction and discussion in the classroom;
- facilitating experiential learning through overseas visits or visits to local diverse communities;
- introducing the idea of internationalisation and help students understand the relevance to their subject;
- utilising a student mentoring or buddy system. (Simm and Marvell, 2017; Heffernan et al., 2019; Fragouli, 2020)

With global and societal changes an internationalised curriculum will be needed to support employability.

Embedding employability skills

The employability agenda has been driven by changes to university funding, widening participation, and increasing use of league tables and metrics such as the graduate outcomes survey (Higher Education Statistics Agency, 2021). Universities are under increasing pressure to produce employable graduates, which are ready for modern work practices. This is challenging in the current work environment with the increases in the use of technology and remote working. To keep up with the rapidly changing climate programmes will need to be flexible and use different initiatives in order to be responsive in producing work ready graduates (Tibby and Norton, 2020). The Future of Jobs report 2020 identified the skills which employers will require include critical thinking and analysis, problem-solving, self-management, resilience, stress tolerance, and flexibility (World Economic Forum, 2020). Employability is dynamic and complex, universities will be preparing students for jobs that do not currently exist using technologies that have not been invented (Römgens et al., 2020). The recent coronavirus pandemic resulted in a large drop in graduate recruitment in 2020, putting further emphasis on the need of graduates to identify and generate new opportunities and be flexible to find a graduate-level position (High Fliers, 2021). Students worry about getting into employment once they graduate so the more employability skills they can develop, the better prepared and confident they will be (Office for Students, 2021).

The skills and attributes required by the graduates are described in various ways including generic competencies, soft skills, key competencies, transferable skills, employability skills, graduate attributes, and many variants of these terms. These are skills that help graduates to create working relationships and throughout this chapter the term used for these will be employability skills. The skills required to help a graduate to thrive in a professional environment. Employability is more than just getting a job; it is about developing students into well-rounded individuals who are adaptable and enterprising (Wolff and Booth, 2017). There continue to be concerns about the gap between higher education and the requirements of employers. These concerns have prompted national and institutional policy and guidance (Advance HE, 2021).

It is important to engage with students, employers, and other stakeholders in identifying priorities for your programme. Principles set down by the Advance HE (2021) include students having an opportunity to develop the skills knowledge and attributes, having a collaborative approach to learning and teaching, a culture of employability, and effective collaboration with employers. Tibby and Norton (2020, p. 8) suggest a series of questions for defining employability which would be helpful to review when developing your programme. These are quoted below:

1. What does employability mean to you, your team, and stakeholders?
2. What does your industry sector, employers, professional bodies, or area of practice want to see in graduates?
3. Are your graduates meeting their requirements?
4. Are there areas they believe are lacking in graduates?
5. Do you address these?
6. Should these be addressed through the curriculum, through extra-curricular activities, or both?
7. What are the students' expectations of how you can enhance their employability? How are your students engaged with employability?
8. Can you agree on a working model/definition for employability in your context?

Developing employability skills is much more than the centralised specialists for in careers and employment. Ideally, employability will be integrated into the design of the curriculum because while student services are a valuable resource, they cannot fully meet the needs of the student's development. You should consider how you are going to engage students with their employability, both within the curriculum and with extracurricular activities. One of your roles as programme leader will be to encourage students to take ownership of their employability and help them understand their learning and how this is transferable because some students have difficulty identifying and understanding employability skills (Okolie et al., 2020).

Three different mechanisms for improving employability skills have been identified: teaching and assessment of employability skills, employer involvement in programme design and delivery, and students participating in work experience (Mason et al., 2009). Employability skills cannot be effectively developed within a classroom situation (Cranmer, 2006; Virtanen and Tynjälä, 2018). Students need to be exposed to authentic practices; this can be through either practical experience or simulation, somewhere where they can put theory into context (Virtanen and Tynjälä, 2018). Incorporating opportunities for work experience is an effective way for students to develop employability skills (Monteiro et al., 2020). The Covid-19 pandemic brought significant changes in working arrangements. This will have an impact on some students experiencing face-to-face working environments. The hybrid of remote working and working on location is likely to remain for some time. A student's work experience may also be a hybrid that seeks to replicate an authentic workplace. The skills required for this flexible working will need to be incorporated into those traditionally recognised (Gill, 2018). Student placements are discussed further in Chapter 7.

Active learning and the use of assessments that require the deployment of some employability skills can aid students' development (Okolie et al., 2020). Social skills can be developed through activities that facilitate the socialisation and interaction of students both between themselves and with teachers (Okolie et al., 2020). You should therefore incorporate situations into the programme that require collaboration and interaction (Virtanen and Tynjälä, 2018). Internships can form a bridge between education and employment. Steps need to be made to address the social inequality associated with internships which can be socially exclusive, with students having the opportunity of internships being influenced by their resources and class background (Cullinane and Montacute, 2018). With the challenges of finding internships, innovative strategies may be needed to provide the student experience such as the example of students as lecturers providing meaningful work experience within the educational setting (Ellidge and Griffiths, 2021). Simulation requiring the application of employability skills can be used to provide a safe environment in which students can explore new ideas and where deep reflection can be facilitated (Virtanen and Tynjälä, 2018). There are also examples of the use of problem-based learning to develop employability skills and competencies (Mekovec et al., 2018; Pardo-Garcia and Barac, 2020). Alumni can be a valuable resource for students to learn from (Tibby and Norton, 2020). Discussing the experiences of past and present students in terms of employment can provide effective peer learning. Peer assessment has been identified as having potential for developing employability skills (Cassidy, 2006; Virtanen and Tynjälä, 2018). This increases students' responsibility and autonomy, gives insight into the expectations for high-quality work, has a positive effect on students' motivation to study, provides an effective way of increasing feedback, and encourages deeper learning. An example from Australia is the development forum which enables graduating students to engage with people from industry (Gill, 2018). This involves an annual one-day student workshop bringing together students and enabling them to network with leaders from the industry. Initiatives like these can help to plug the gaps which curriculum content may struggle to fill. However, some initiatives involve a selective process with students applying to be involved. There is no question that these initiatives benefit the students taking part, but any selective process can result in less proactive students missing out. Extracurricular activity does have its place and it is important to consider that different students within the same programme might benefit from different interventions as individuals do not develop their employability skills in the same way. Therefore, you should have a student-centred approach to employability skills (Monteiro et al., 2020). Embedding employability skills is all about preparing the students for a future workforce and cultural changes. Academics, support staff, careers services, student services, the Union of Students, and employers all have a role to play in embedding employability into the culture of the institution (Tibby and Norton, 2020).

Summary

This chapter has focused on approaches you can use when designing your programme. It started by discussing your role in the process of programme validation and tips that you may find helpful for fulfilling your role. Engagement with stakeholders is an essential part of designing a programme. You are prompted to think about who this might be for your programme. Co-creation of your programme, particularly with students, will enhance your programme. This concept along with practical guidance and questions are included to aid your reflection of using co-creation to develop your curriculum. The involvement of other stakeholders from placement providers, employers and people using their services all need to be involved in the development of a programme to ensure it is fit for its purpose. The second part of the chapter explores change management. Starting with curriculum justification and situation it is followed by techniques that you can use for consultation. Vignettes describe how programme leaders have used some of these techniques. The final part of the chapter explores some of the major themes you need to consider when developing your programme, including education for sustainable development, internationalising your curricular, and embedding employability skills.

References

Advance HE, 2021. Embedding employability in higher education. Available from https://www.advance-he.ac.uk/guidance/teaching-and-learning/embedding-employability (accessed 17 October 2021).

Advance HE and Quality Assurance Agency, 2021. Education for sustainable development guidance. Available from https://www.qaa.ac.uk/quality-code/education-for-sustainable-development (accessed 17 October 2021).

Allen, J., Dyas, J. and Jones, M., 2004. Building consensus in health care: A guide to using the nominal group technique. *British Journal of Community Nursing*, 9(3), pp. 110–114.

Annan-Diab, F. and Molinari, C., 2017. Interdisciplinarity: Practical approach to advancing education for sustainability and for the Sustainable Development Goals. *The International Journal of Management Education*, 15(2), pp. 73–83.

Ávila, L.V., Leal Filho, W., Brandli, L., Macgregor, C.J., Molthan-Hill, P., Özuyar, P. G., and Moreira, R.M., 2017. Barriers to innovation and sustainability at universities around the world. *Journal of Cleaner Production*, 164, pp. 1268–1278.

Bovill, C., 2019. Student–staff partnerships in learning and teaching: An overview of current practice and discourse. *Journal of Geography in Higher Education*, 43(4), pp. 385–398.

Bovill, C., 2020. Co-creation in learning and teaching: The case for a whole-class approach in higher education. *Higher Education*, 79(6), pp. 1023–1037.

Bovill, C. and Woolmer, C., 2019. How conceptualisations of curriculum in higher education influence student–staff co-creation in and of the curriculum. *Higher Education*, 78(3), pp. 407–422.

Cameron, A., 2018. Embedding race equality and internationalising the curriculum: Abertay University case study. Available from https://s3.eu-west-2.amazonaws.com/assets.creode.advancehe-document-manager/documents/hea/private/hub/download/Abertay%20EEDC%20SEP%20Case%20study_1568037587.pdf (accessed 17 October 2021).

Carney, O., McIntosh, J., and Worth, A., 1996. The use of the nominal group technique in research with community nurses. *Journal of Advanced Nursing*, 23(5), pp. 1024–1029.

Carter, C. and Brown, K., 2014. Service user input in pre-registration children's nursing education. *Nursing Children and Young People*, 26(4), pp. 28–31.

Cassidy, S., 2006. Developing employability skills: Peer assessment in higher education. *Education+ training*, 48(7), pp. 508–517.

Castiglioni, A., Shewchuk, R.M., Willett, L.L., Heudebert, G.R., and Centor, R.M., 2008. A pilot study using nominal group technique to assess residents' perceptions of successful attending rounds. *Journal of General Internal Medicine*, 23(7), pp. 1060–1065.

Clifford, V.A., 2009. Engaging the disciplines in internationalising the curriculum. *International Journal for Academic Development*, 14(2), pp. 133–143.

Coetzer, A. and Sitlington, H., 2014. What knowledge, skills and attitudes should strategic HRM students acquire? A Delphi study. *Asia Pacific Journal of Human Resources*, 52(2), pp. 155–172.

Cook-Sather, A., 2020. Respecting voices: How the co-creation of teaching and learning can support academic staff, underrepresented students, and equitable practices. *Higher Education*, 79(5), pp. 885–901.

Cranmer, S., 2006. Enhancing graduate employability: Best intentions and mixed outcomes. *Studies in Higher Education*, 31(2), pp. 169–184.

Cullinane, C. and Montacute, R., 2018. Pay as you go? Internship pay, quality and access in the graduate jobs market. Available from https://www.suttontrust.com/our-research/internships-pay-as-you-go/ (accessed 17 October 2021).

Delbecq, A.L., Van de Ven, A.H., and Gustafson, D.H., 1975. *Group techniques for program planning: A guide to nominal group and Delphi processes.* Scott, Foresman.

De Ruyter, K., 1996. Focus versus nominal group interviews: A comparative analysis. *Marketing Intelligence & Planning*, 14(6), pp. 44–50.

de Wit, H., 2019. Internationalization in higher education, a critical review. *SFU Educational Review*, 12(3), pp. 9–17.

Dobbie, A., Rhodes, M., Tysinger, J.W., and Freeman, J., 2004. Using a modified nominal group technique as a curriculum evaluation tool. *Family Medicine*, 36, pp. 402–406.

Doyle, E., Buckley, P., and McCarthy, B., 2021. The impact of content co-creation on academic achievement. *Assessment & Evaluation in Higher Education*, 46(3), pp. 494–507.

El Enany, N., Currie, G., and Lockett, A., 2013. A paradox in healthcare service development: Professionalization of service users. *Social Science & Medicine*, 80, pp. 24–30.

Ellidge, D. and Griffiths, L., 2021. Students as Lecturers: developing skills for graduate roles. In Norton, S. and Dalyrymple, R. (eds), *Employability: Breaking the mould: A case study compendium*. Advance HE.

Fragouli, E., 2020. A critical discussion on issues of higher education: Curriculum internationalization, challenges, and opportunities. *International Journal of Education and Learning*, 2, pp. 67–75.

Gallagher, M., Hares, T.I.M., Spencer, J., Bradshaw, C., and Webb, I.A.N., 1993. The nominal group technique: A research tool for general practice? *Family Practice*, 10 (1), pp. 76–81.

Gaskin, S., 2003. A guide to Nominal Group Technique (NGT) in focus-group research. *Journal of Geography in Higher Education*, 27(3), pp. 342–347.

Gill, R., 2018. Building employability skills for higher education students: An Australian example. *Journal of Teaching and Learning for Graduate Employability*, 9(1), pp. 84–92.

Green, R.A. 2014. *The Delphi technique in educational research.* SAGE.

Green, W., 2019. Engaging "students as partners" in global learning: Some possibilities and provocations. *Journal of Studies in International Education*, 23(1), pp. 10–29.

Green, W. and Mertova, P., 2016. Transformalists and transactionists: Towards a more comprehensive understanding of academics' engagement with 'internationalisation of the curriculum'. *Research in Comparative and International Education*, 11(3), pp. 229–246.

Gupta, U.G. and Clarke, R.E., 1996. Theory and applications of the Delphi technique: A bibliography (1975–1994). *Technological Forecasting and Social Change*, 53(2), pp. 185–211.

Health and Care Professions Council, 2018. Service user and carer involvement. Available from https://www.hcpc-uk.org/education/resources/education-standards/service-user-and-carer-involvement/ (accessed 17 October 2021).

Heffernan, T., Morrison, D., Magne, P., Payne, S., and Cotton, D., 2019. Internalising internationalisation: Views of internationalisation of the curriculum among non-mobile home students. *Studies in Higher Education*, 44(12), pp. 2359–2373.

Higher Education Statistics Agency, 2021. HE graduate outcomes data. Available from https://www.hesa.ac.uk/data-and-analysis/graduates (accessed 17 October 2021).

High Fliers, 2021. The graduate market. Available from https://www.highfliers.co.uk/download/2021/graduate_market/GM21-Report.pdf (accessed 17 October 2021).

Hsu, W.L., Chen, Y.S., Shiau, Y.C., Liu, H.L., and Chern, T.Y., 2019. Curriculum design in construction engineering departments for colleges in Taiwan. *Education Sciences*, 9(1). doi:10.3390/educsci9010065.

Jones, E., 2017. Internationalisation of the curriculum: Challenges, misconceptions and the role of disciplines. In H. Casper-Hehne and T. Reiffenrath (eds), *Internationalisierung der Curricula an Hochschulen: Konzepte, Initiativen, Maßnahmen*, pp. 21–38. W. Bertelsmann Verlag (wbv).

Jones, E. and Killick, D., 2013. Graduate attributes and the internationalized curriculum: Embedding a global outlook in disciplinary learning outcomes. *Journal of Studies in International Education*, 17(2), pp. 165–182.

Kemp, S (2015). *Teaching sustainability development e-book: Tutor resources and student activity series.* Advance HE. Available from https://www.advance-he.ac.uk/knowledge-hub/teaching-sustainable-development-ebook-tutor-resource-student-activity-series (accessed 1 March 2021).

Kidd, P.S. and Parshall, M.B., 2000. Getting the focus and the group: Enhancing analytical rigor in focus group research. *Qualitative Health Research*, 10(3), pp. 293–308.

Kiely, R., 2003. What works for you? A group discussion approach to programme evaluation. *Studies in Educational Evaluation*, 29(4), pp. 293–314.

Lancaster, T., Hart, R., and Gardner, S., 2002. Literature and medicine: Evaluating a special study module using the nominal group technique. *Medical Education*, 36 (11), pp. 1071–1076.

Leal Filho, W., Raath, S., Lazzarini, B., Vargas, V.R., de Souza, L., Anholon, R., Quelhas, O.L.G., Haddad, R., Klavins, M., and Orlovic, V.L., 2018. The role of transformation in learning and education for sustainability. *Journal of Cleaner Production*, 199, pp. 286–295.

Leask, B., 2015. *Internationalizing the curriculum.* Routledge.

Leicht, A., Heiss, J., and Byun, W.J., 2018. *Issues and trends in education for sustainable development* (Vol. 5). UNESCO Publishing.

Lloyd-Jones, G., Fowell, S., and Bligh, J.G., 1999. *The use of the nominal group technique as an evaluative tool in medical undergraduate education. Medical Education*, 33(1), pp. 8–13.

Lozano, R., Merrill, M.Y., Sammalisto, K., Ceulemans, K., and Lozano, F.J., 2017. Connecting competences and pedagogical approaches for sustainable development in higher education: A literature review and framework proposal. *Sustainability*, 9 (10), p. 1889. doi:10.3390/su9101889

Lubicz-Nawrocka, T.M., 2018. Students as partners in learning and teaching: The benefits of co-creation of the curriculum. *International Journal for Students as Partners*, 2(1), pp. 47–63.

Marinoni, G., 2019. *Internationalization of higher education: An evolving landscape, locally and globally: IAU 5th Global Survey*. DUZ Verlags-und Medienhaus GmbH.

Mason, G., Williams, G. and Cranmer, S., 2009. Employability skills initiatives in higher education: What effects do they have on graduate labour market outcomes? *Education Economics*, 17(1), pp. 1–30.

Masters, H., Forrest, S., Harley, A., Hunter, M., Brown, N., and Risk, I., 2002. Involving mental health service users and carers in curriculum development: Moving beyond 'classroom' involvement. *Journal of Psychiatric and Mental Health Nursing*, 9(3), pp. 309–316.

Mekovec, R., Aničić, K.P. and Arbanas, K., 2018. Developing undergraduate IT students' generic competencies through problem-based learning. *TEM Journal*, 7(1), pp. 193–200.

Monteiro, S., Almeida, L., Gomes, C., and Sinval, J., 2020. Employability profiles of higher education graduates: A person-oriented approach. *Studies in Higher Education*, pp. 1–14.

Murphy, R., Nixon, S., Brooman, S., and Fearon, D., 2017. 'I am wary of giving too much power to students': Addressing the 'but' in the principle of staff–student partnership. *International Journal for Students as Partners*, 1(1), 1–16.

National Health Service Institute for Innovation and Improvement, 2008. The organising for Quality and Value: Delivering Improvement Programme. Available from https://www.england.nhs.uk/improvement-hub/wp-content/uploads/sites/44/2018/06/Engaging-Involving-Understanding-Others-Perspectives.pdf (accessed 17 October 2021).

Nursing and Midwifery Council, 2018. Standards framework for nursing and midwifery education. Available from https://www.nmc.org.uk/standards-for-education-and-training/standards-framework-for-nursing-and-midwifery-education/ (accessed 17 October 2021).

Office for Students, 2021. Graduate employment and skills guide. Available from https://www.officeforstudents.org.uk/for-students/student-outcomes-and-employability/graduate-employment-and-skills-guide/ (accessed 17 October 2021).

Okolie, U.C., Igwe, P.A., Nwosu, H.E., Eneje, B.C., and Mlanga, S., 2020. Enhancing graduate employability: Why do higher education institutions have problems with teaching generic skills? *Policy Futures in Education*, 18(2), pp. 294–313.

Pardo-Garcia, C. and Barac, M., 2020. Promoting employability in higher education: A case study on boosting entrepreneurship skills. *Sustainability*, 12(10). doi:10.3390/su12104004.

Perry, J. and Linsley, S., 2006. The use of the nominal group technique as an evaluative tool in the teaching and summative assessment of the inter-personal skills of student mental health nurses. *Nurse Education Today*, 26(4), pp. 346–353.

Quality Assurance Agency, 2018. UK Quality Code for Higher Education Advice and Guidance Course Design and Development. Available from file:///Users/sarahnaylor/Downloads/advice-and-guidance-course-design-and-development.pdf (accessed 17 October 2021).

Rajhans, V., Rege, S., Memon, U., and Shinde, A., 2020. Adopting a modified Delphi technique for revisiting the curriculum: A useful approach during the COVID-19 pandemic. *Qualitative Research Journal*, 20(4), pp. 373–382.

Römgens, I., Scoupe, R., and Beausaert, S., 2020. Unraveling the concept of employability, bringing together research on employability in higher education and the workplace. *Studies in Higher Education*, 45(12), pp. 2588–2603.

Ryan, D., Faulkner, F., Dillane, D., and Flood, R.V., 2021. Communities of practice as a solution for the implementation gap in internationalisation of the curriculum. *Higher Education Research & Development*, pp. 1–16. DOI: doi:10.1080/07294360.2021.1877630.

Selby, D., 2009. Towards the sustainability university: The Centre for Sustainable Futures, University of Plymouth . *Journal of Education for Sustainable Development*, 3(1), pp. 103–106.

Simm, D. and Marvell, A., 2017. Creating global students: Opportunities, challenges and experiences of internationalizing the geography curriculum in higher education. *Journal of Geography in Higher Education*, 41(4), pp. 467–474. DOI: doi:10.1080/03098265.2017.1373332.

Sterling, S. ed., 2010. *Sustainability education: Perspectives and practice across higher education*. Taylor & Francis.

Steward, B., 2001. Using nominal group technique to explore competence in occupational therapy and physiotherapy students during first-year placements. *British Journal of Occupational Therapy*, 64(6), pp. 298–304.

Students Organising for Sustainability, 2021. Available from https://www.sos-uk.org/ (accessed 17 October 2021).

Taylor, C.A. and Bovill, C., 2018. Towards an ecology of participation: Process philosophy and co-creation of higher education curricula. *European Educational Research Journal*, 17(1), pp. 112–128.

Tibby, M. and Norton, S., 2020Essential frameworks for enhancing student success: embedding employability. Available from https://www.advance-he.ac.uk/knowledge-hub/essential-frameworks-enhancing-student-success-embedding-employability (accessed 17 October 2021).

United Nations, 2021. The 17 Goals. Available from https://sdgs.un.org/goals (accessed 17 October 2021).

United Nations Educational, Scientific and Cultural Organisation, 2021. Sustainable Development Goals – Resources for educators. Available from https://en.unesco.org/themes/education/sdgs/material (accessed 17 October 2021).

Van de Ven, A.H. and Delbecq, A.L., 1974. The effectiveness of nominal, Delphi, and interacting group decision making processes. *Academy of Management Journal*, 17 (4), pp. 605–621.

Virtanen, A. and Tynjälä, P., 2018. Factors explaining the learning of generic skills: A study of university students' experiences. *Teaching in Higher Education*, 24(7), pp. 880–894.

Wijaya Mulya, T., 2019. Contesting the neoliberalisation of higher education through student–faculty partnership. *International Journal for Academic Development*, 24(1), pp. 86–90.

Williams, P.L., White, N., Klem, R., Wilson, S.E., and Bartholomew, P., 2006. Clinical education and training: Using the nominal group technique in research with radiographers to identify factors affecting quality and capacity. *Radiography*, 12(3), pp. 215–224.

Wolff, R. and Booth, M., 2017. Bridging the gap: Creating a new approach for assuring 21st century employability skills. *Change: The Magazine of Higher Learning*, 49(6), pp. 51–54.

World Economic Forum, 2020. The Future of Jobs report. Available from https://www3.weforum.org/docs/WEF_Future_of_Jobs_2020.pdf (accessed 17 October 2021).

5 Student experience

Mental well-being

The mental health of students in higher education is high on the agenda across the world. This will encompass both academic and non-academic domains of a student's life and is something that should be considered by programme leaders (Hewitt, 2019). Data on the mental well-being of the population is collected (Hewitt, 2019). The indication that mental health issues are higher in the student population than in the general population cannot be ignored. It is concerning that suicides among higher education students have been estimated at 4.7 per 100,000 students (Office for National Statistics, 2018), although this is lower than the national average for England and Wales in 2020 of 10 per 100,000 (Office for National Statistics, 2021). Changes in study patterns as a result of the pandemic are likely to remain for some time and the impact of this is yet to be realised. A survey of nearly 50,000 students undertaken in America showed an increase in students' mental ill-health as a result of the pandemic (Chirikov et al., 2020). This is likely to be replicated across continents. Guidance is available but much of this focuses on an institutional level, student support services, and student initiatives. However, programme leaders have an important role in mental well-being.

There is no single cause of mental ill-health and therefore no one solution (Schreiber, 2018). Mental well-being should not be seen as a separate issue within your programme, behaviours associated with mental well-being can be promoted throughout the programme such as through lectures and seminars, extracurricular activities, and initiatives (Sarmento, 2015). Students may enter the programme with pre-existing diagnosis of mental health issues and be reluctant to disclose concerns about their mental health due to the associated stigma and possible discrimination (Martin, 2010; Laidlaw et al., 2016). It is important to be able to identify students and liaise with support services to be able to put support in place. Everyone has a role in breaking the silence around mental health and reducing the stigma that can be associated with it. Yet an anonymous survey at one university identified that around two-thirds of students did not disclose their mental health condition to staff (Martin, 2010). Schreiber (2018) cautions against a paternalistic approach to mental

DOI: 10.4324/9781003126355-6

well-being but to collaborate with students and ensure they are active participants.

Your programme cannot and should not be completely sanitised of challenges that may be uncomfortable or even stressful (Schreiber, 2018). But you can create an environment that is inclusive, caring, compassionate, and supportive. Whilst a programme leader cannot act *in loco parentis* it is valuable to have a system by which you can be alerted to any students who may be experiencing mental health issues. This is not so that you can address any issues either personally or through their personal tutor, but that you can signpost students to available interventions. You should make sure that your personal tutors know where to signpost students (Chirikov et al., 2020). Services within universities themselves differ greatly in the types of support on offer. You should proactively publicise the resources available through a variety of modes of communication (Chirikov et al., 2020). This should be done as soon as student induction so they are aware of these as soon as they start their programme. It has been suggested that students access services when their mental well-being is affecting their ability to cope (Broglia et al., 2018). Early identification and signposting can prevent the deterioration of a student's situation (Chirikov et al., 2020). Using a variety of platforms such as WhatsApp, text, email, social media, and out-of-office responses means that the information is readily available rather than students needing to hunt for where to obtain support in moments of crisis.

The main stressors are likely to be exams, assignments, workload, and placement (Deasy et al., 2014). You can help to reduce these through clear information about the programme; for example, about assignment deadlines which will encourage forward planning and reduce the 'fear of the unknown'. Processes for monitoring engagement are important because signs to look out for amongst your students are erratic attendance, lack of participation, withdrawal from social activity, and symptoms of ill health (Rückert, 2015). Students have different ways of coping, some choosing positive actions, others use maladaptive strategies through their eating habits, alcohol consumption, or substance use (Reavley and Jorm, 2010). Some students isolate themselves from others when stressed, and denial can occur when students are reticent to admit to themselves or others that they may be struggling (Deasy et al., 2014). Placements can be a key stressor for students (Deasy et al., 2014). It is, therefore, important to consider the mental well-being of students whilst they are working remote from the university. Take into consideration their workplace experience alongside their academic workload. Another group of students who may need additional support is international students (Rückert, 2015). This was particularly important whilst universities were closing campuses and international students are living away from their usual support mechanisms (Sahu, 2020). The recent closure of campuses during the pandemic has caused major disruption and additional stressors for students.

The Higher Education Academy promotes embedding mental well-being in the content of the curriculum (Houghton and Anderson, 2017). Not just within health and well-being, but exploring where it can be placed within the content of all disciplines. The idea of curriculum infusion, in which real-life values and situations such as alcohol abuse, conflict resolution, and mental well-being are strategically included in curricula, is gaining interest (Kenney and Grim, 2015). Houghton and Anderson (2017) provide ideas about how this can be achieved.

- Look at the barriers to embedding mental well-being into your curriculum.
- Provide a positive learning environment where positive mental well-being is overtly included.
- Consider your own mental well-being and how this may impact on the students.
- Explore the benefits that inter-disciplinary connections can have on mental well-being.
- Embed mental well-being resources into your curriculum.
- Consider using the 'five ways to well-being' as a framework to support student' well-being.

You should encourage your students to be active partners in creating conditions conducive to mental well-being (Schreiber, 2018). MIND in partnership with Goldman Sachs developed a mentally healthy universities programme aimed at improving staff and student well-being (MIND, 2021). Their student hub provides tips for taking care of one's mental health including five ways to well-being: connect, be active, learn, take notice, and give (MIND, 2021).

Connect

Programme leaders can help to facilitate some of these; for example, by helping students connect both with other students and with staff at the university. This can be achieved through a variety of means such as the use of group assessment to encourage study groups. Some students are often reluctant to speak about experiencing problems and if they do they will initially go to someone whom they know well (Laidlaw et al., 2016). This is likely to be family and friends (Martin, 2010; Reavley and Jorm, 2010). There are initiatives that you can signpost your students to such as the 'Look after your mate' which aims to empower students to support their friends whilst looking after their own well-being (Student Minds, 2021a). Explore and discuss with the delivery team the use of interactive teaching and learning strategies to help students integrate. This is even more important with remote teaching where face contact and socialisation are limited.

Be active

You can help students to be more active by encouraging them to move around during and between sessions. You could, for example, when taking a break in a lecture, or student meeting encourage students to engage in activity and give feedback on what they have done during the break. This is particularly important if the session is being delivered remotely with students sitting at a computer. In addition, you can encourage extracurricular activities for students on your programme such as lunchtime walks. You can promote 'get active' campaigns and encourage students to share their progress via social media.

Learn

Learning is one of the five ways to well-being. However, it has to be learning that is valuable to the individual. Students may question the value of some modules and assessments (Deasy et al., 2014). Learning can be both a source of stress but also conducive to enhancing self-esteem leading to mental well-being. As programme leader, you have an overview of the whole student journey to be able to facilitate a positive learning environment. You have an overview of the whole programme, and it is important to look at the student experience in relation to their workload. There may for example be overlap of content between modules, bunching of assessment or duplication of assessment in some content of the programme. This is not always evident if modules are looked at in isolation. Laidlaw et al. (2016) identify two sources of stress: short-term caused by exams or submission deadlines; and long-term brought on by the transition into university. You should also look at the timing and deployment of feedback which can be a major source of anxiety for students. Using a feed-forward approach will soften the blow of any negative feedback that maybe necessary for some students. Also, examine your students' experience of their transition onto your programme and what you can do to facilitate a smooth transition.

Take notice

Within your programme you can encourage self-reflection and students to 'take notice'. Gaining popularity is the use of mindfulness which is a strategy that you can promote amongst your students. This encourages people to pay attention to the present and can improve mental well-being. It is recommended by the National Institute of Health and Care Excellence (NICE) and can be incorporated into everyday teaching practice (Bush, 2011; Schwind et al., 2017; Ergas and Hadar, 2021). Encourage your students not just to see their learning in isolation but to take notice and consider how this connects with various aspects of their life and their community.

Give

The fifth way, give, is about participating in social and community life, helping others, and committing acts of kindness. The sense of belonging generated by being part of a student community can have a positive effect on mental well-being (Laidlaw et al., 2016). There are various ways within your programme that you can facilitate this. Group work, peer mentoring, peer tutoring, peer feedback are all ways that enable students to give back to their fellow students.

It is important for you as a programme leader to understand mental well-being, the indicators of mental ill-health, and the coping behaviours of students (Rückert, 2015). This way you are better able to recognise and support students in difficulty. A short mental health first-aid course can give you greater confidence in being able to provide help for your students who are struggling with their mental well-being (Reavley and Jorm, 2010). Other resources are available around providing metal health support for students (Office for Students, 2021; The Wellbeing Thesis, 2021).

Use the questions in the box below to help you reflect on how you can improve mental well-being within your programme.

Reflection

- What do you understand about mental well-being? What are the risk factors and coping strategies of your students?
- What facilities are available within your university? Do you know where you can signpost your students to get help and support?
- Where can you infuse mental well-being into your curriculum?
- Closely examine your students' experience. Is there any bunching or overlap of assessment? Is the relevance of all the content explicit?
- What extracurricular activities are available within your university that promote mental well-being? How can you signpost your students to these?

Specific interventions

Personal tutoring

Programme leaders have an important role in ensuring an effective, equitable personal tutoring scheme is in place. You may, or may not, undertake the role of personal tutor for students on your programme, but you may need to support those who are personal tutors for your students. Nationally personal tutoring is considered to be important for the student experience and impact on student retention (National Union of Students, 2015). Within different institutions, the role of the personal tutor can vary on a scale between academic advisor and pastoral care, running alongside a variety of centrally based student support mechanisms. Looking at university strategies it is apparent that some universities put value on personal tutoring, but from experience some universities have a strategy that is not fully implemented. Challenges exist in delivering personal tutoring, whether it is a directive approach with issues around timetabled sessions, or a more flexible approach which can lead to personal tutoring being too passive. Some universities put such emphasis on the need for attending personal tutoring sessions that sanctions can be initiated for non-attendance at scheduled sessions. Showing similar conviction others provide prescriptive agendas for personal tutor meetings. Several put emphasis on the personal tutor arranging the meetings. Some institutions stipulate that personal tutoring should be on a one-to-one basis. However, personal tutoring can be conducted as a group.

The personal tutor is the best person to provide support for students during work-based placements (Gidman, 2001; Braine and Parnell, 2011), therefore resulting in personal tutoring at a distance. Jelfs et al. (2009) explored what constitutes good tutoring in distance learning. Aspects that emerged were: the development of critical thinking, vocational guidance, subject specialism promoting student interaction and pastoral care. Personal tutors support students in personal development planning and the development of skills relevant to the workplace (Clegg and Bufton, 2008). In addition the personal tutor may help students to fit into their placement organisation, helping them to adapt to the culture of the workplace and develop conducive behaviours, values, and attitudes (Cottrell, 2015).

The massification and widening participation in higher education has led to an increase in the staff student ratios and greater diversity (Stephen et al., 2008). This wider access and diverse student population leads to variations in their preparedness for university, making the role of the personal tutor more vital than ever, as a means of student support (Stevenson, 2009). However, meeting the demands of the student can result in personal tutors feeling overwhelmed and anxious (Stephen et al., 2008). A personal tutor's competence and confidence are key to effective personal tutoring (McFarlane, 2016). This competence and confidence can develop experientially over time, but need facilitating through peer support and training (McFarlane, 2016). One way to provide this is to have regular meetings where the team get together and discuss each student in relation to attendance, placement, and any issues that need addressing. This provides a platform for academic peer support in a confidential environment. It ensures that each student is visible as a person and less likely to get 'lost in the system'. Where programmes are large or dispersed an alternative possibly virtual mechanism for highlighting and discussing students who are experiencing issues will be useful.

Students do not seek help for all sorts of reasons, including feeling 'ashamed' that they are not doing it themselves (Clegg and Bufton, 2008), or worrying about taking their tutors' time (Stephen et al., 2008; Braine and Parnell, 2011). They may also see academic staff as unapproachable. The student–tutor relationship will be improved by being approachable; knowing the student's name, saying hello if meeting on campus, and stopping to chat (Hagenauer and Volet, 2014). There is concern that in being too approachable personal tutors may be swamped by requests from students which adds to their workload, but this can be identified at staff meetings and managed (Stephen et al., 2008).

Scheduled sessions should facilitate the building of a good relationship between student and personal tutor, in which they develop mutual rapport, a sense of belonging, and feel valued (Braine and Parnell, 2011). This is important because the quality of the relationship, particularly in terms of accessibility and approachability, impacts on the ability of a struggling student to remain on the programme (Braine and Parnell, 2011). Some students may not know how to take up the offer of ambiguous 'drop-in' sessions and would be better having pre-booked arrangements (Clegg and Bufton, 2008). Whilst students recognise that they are expected to be independent learners at university they would also like their tutor to be proactive in their development (Stephen et al., 2008). Structured support, particularly in groups, can foster a sense of belonging and develop employability skills such as learning from each other (Braine and Parnell, 2011).

As programme leader you may find that many student issues come through you. Being a personal tutor in itself can be emotionally challenging and you will be exposed to more student issues than a personal tutor (Luck, 2010). For your own health and well-being, you need to have boundaries in dealing with the plethora of personal issues that students presented with. Being supportive and directing students to other services is what is required, rather than problem-solving or nurturing.

There are many different models of personal tutoring. What works well is a *directive* approach, particularly initially at the start of the programme (Young et al., 2005). This approach is useful to start with because students do not always know what they need, or when they need it. They often feel that they should 'soldier on'. In addition, for the personal tutor to be effective, they need to build a relationship with the student (Dobinson-Harrington, 2006; Neville 2007). Once this has been achieved, a shift to the more *responsive* model could be made.

The vignettes below provide examples of students' interactions with their personal tutors. Consider how you would support your personal tutors in a similar situation.

Vignette

A second-year student experienced the loss of a family member. He had time away from the programme and accessed specialist bereavement counselling outside of the university. The student was keen to return to university and it was then that personal tutoring was required. I met with the student in a small private room to chat about catching up on missed work.

He was very keen to return to his year group and not take any further time off or delay his qualification. We discussed practical issues around catching up on topics missed at university and missed time on placement. He expressed concerns about returning to placement. It was at this point that I became aware through his body language that he was becoming emotional. So, I paused the conversation, which was taking a practical approach, to allow him to discuss his feelings and concerns. Once I allowed the time and opportunity he freely talked about his experience and concerns with minimal prompting via the occasional verbal and non-verbal communication on my part. I felt it was important to allow the student time and not rush ahead making assumptions about his state of mind.

It was important to help the student to understand his situation and for this to inform his choices. Once we both had a better picture of the issues around returning to placement we discussed the options, including the ability to temporarily withdraw from university which he reiterated that he was not wanting to do. The university has simulation facilities and when this was suggested as a first step to returning to placement he was unsure about the potential to help but agreed to try this strategy. A date was arranged for this.

Being mindful of the limitations of the personal tutor role and that other central support is available I considered the need for a referral. It was quite apparent that this student needed expert help and possibly further bereavement counselling. He also needed the organisational support regarding extension to assignments, etc. Thus, I suggested that he arranged to see the student support officer, who could more thoroughly assess his needs. I gained the student's permission to talk to the student support officer about his issues.

One positive aspect of this encounter is that it was held in a private room. Some tutor sessions are held in a more open environment. This event highlights that issues raised by the students and their emotional responses can be unpredictable. In a more public environment the student may not have opened up about his issues leaving them unresolved or in him being embarrassed by his emotions. Good communication skills, particularly listening skills, are essential.

This student needed practical and emotional support to complete the programme. Sometimes students do not fully understand the reasoning behind the options available and as in this case it is important to give them choices and try to explain as fully as possible the reasons and potential outcomes of the opportunities available. It is important to understand the limitations of my role as a programme leader. I do not have the expert skills of a counsellor that this student required, and it is necessary to know what other support mechanisms are available.

Vignette

One of my students had failed the first attempt in an assignment and the meeting I am reflecting on was held during the referral period. She had ignored any emails I had sent and as I had heard from a colleague that she was struggling coming to terms with being referred I thought that we should meet face to face. I discreetly asked her to stay back after one of the small group teaching sessions, which she agreed to do.

I started the conversation asking her how she felt about the assignment. At which point she took out a copy of the draft that she had been working on and asked me what I thought about it. She had a nonchalant manner. The conversation took on a practical approach as we went through the assignment. Gradually the communication barriers began to erode and we could have a more meaningful conversation. It was important in this situation for both the student and I to understand why this assignment had gone so wrong. I asked her what support she had accessed for her assignment. She said that this was mainly though family members so I asked her for more details in order to get a better understanding of her circumstances. I verbally clarified with her that she had a mother with a master's degree and siblings with high-class degrees. I sensed that there was a lot of 'pressure to perform'.

It was important not to appear derogatory about support from family members as this is valuable. However, I stressed that there are variations between universities, particularly regarding referencing styles, and that several options are available for support including the personal tutor, module leader as well as central support via the library. I also talked about my situation of having a son at university and advising him to see his tutors, as giving a little of yourself helps to break down barriers.

I did not think that this student would access face-to-face sessions available through the library for academic writing. However, I made sure that she knew how to access the support available and that support was also available online, which she could access privately. Often, the best person to give academic advice is the personal tutor who has profession-specific knowledge. However, if the student is not receptive to these then other mechanisms need to be offered.

Personally, this was a challenging conversation as the student appeared resentful that she had not passed the assignment. It was important to be led by the student, which I did by starting the conversation by practically discussing the details of the assignment which helped to initiate a two-way conversation. I felt like I was 'treading on egg shells'; that I needed to be very careful about what I said in case I said something that would bring up barriers to the flow of conversation. However, I also felt that it was important to get a better understanding of her situation. I believe that this student was not used to 'failure', that she was proud and had pressure on her to succeed, both from herself and her family. This may have inhibited her asking for support earlier. It is not common practice within my team to have scheduled meetings for academic advisors; these are arranged on an ad hoc basis. For this particular student, a more structured approach would have been more suitable so that the support is accessible without appearing weak by seeking it out.

Peer support

Supportive peer relationships can be considerably successful, reaping benefits for only moderate financial investment from the university. A variety of terminology is used, which can be confusing, including peer mentoring, tutoring, coaching, and peer leaders. The two main terms considered here are peer mentoring, giving social support particularly during the transition into university, and peer tutoring, which provides academic support.

Peer tutoring

Peer tutoring is a method of teaching and learning that, according to Wagner (1982), dates to the evolution of formal teaching, over 300 years BC. Traditionally, peer tutors were assumed to be more experienced than those that they tutor (Tai et al., 2016). However, this has since been refuted as a constraint, and more value has been placed upon the idea of reciprocal learning that occurs amongst peers, supporting benefit in the idea of changing or the switching of roles amongst similar level students (Topping, 1996; Meertens, 2016). This can be applied within the higher education context (Meertens, 2016; Reidlinger et al., 2017). Peer tutoring has been successfully embedded into training programmes for allied health professionals (Meertens, 2016; Bain et al., 2017; Elshami et al., 2020), nursing (Secomb, 2008), and medical students (Field et al., 2007; Bene and Bergus, 2014; Khalid et al., 2018).

Literature suggests multiple benefits exist for the students accepting the role of peer tutor (Secomb, 2008; Parker et al., 2013; Clarke et al., 2019). Through tutoring students develop leadership and communication skills, and learn how to interact with their peers (Secomb, 2008; Clarke et al., 2019). Learning to teach also embeds high levels of conceptual understanding of the subject matter and teaching strategies (Clarke et al., 2019; Parker et al., 2013). Benefits are stated as reciprocal amongst learners. The collective benefits of the group, especially for less-able or average student tutors, can exceed that of more accomplished tutors (Saunders, 1992; Topping, 1996; Secomb, 2008). The process of learning to teach, as well as the act of teaching, creates deep rather than surface-level learning (Saunders, 1992; Secomb, 2008). Peer-tutoring sessions in themselves can improve communication skills in the form of presentation techniques. However, having the opportunity of specific training for this raises the kudos for these students amongst their peers, as well as increasing their own confidence and reducing in-session stressors (Clarke et al., 2019).

Peer mentoring

Peer mentoring is encouraged as a mechanism for supporting the transition into university life. Peer mentors dawn from experienced students can help new students acclimatise to university life and help develop their identity as a student. Peer mentoring can help students develop a sense of belonging, an important factor for student well-being. New students often leave establish support mechanisms and can worry about making friends, a peer mentor can provide a friendly face (Andrews and Clark, 2011). Peer mentoring is being used as a strategy to aid retention and reducing attrition (Collings et al., 2014). Peers are ideally placed to identify and provide support for students who might be floundering and new students may be more willing to approach a mentor than a member of staff (Andrews and Clark, 2011). Peer mentoring has been identified as particularly important for students with additional needs, for example international students (Andrews and Clark, 2011), students with autism (Hamilton et al., 2016; Siew et al., 2017), and refugees (Vickers et al., 2017).

There are many different approaches to peer support. Peer mentoring can be one-to-one or group mentoring, short- or long-term. Some models of peer mentoring are just for the initial few weeks at the start of university life. However, relationships can be built and evolve with prolonged relationships being mutually beneficial well into the first year at university (Andrews and Clark, 2011). A prolonged relationship enables the nurturing of a sense of belonging, helps students to understand what it means to learn at higher level and promotes independent learning. An important factor to consider is whether you have an opt-out programme in which peer mentoring is offered to all students or a self-selecting opt-in programme. The opt-out model sees this mode of support as part of university culture rather than an extra type of support for students in need. Ideally mentoring will be conducted face to face, but currently contact using remote platforms may be necessary.

Benefits to mentors have been identified as developing transferable employability skills including leadership and communication skills (Andrews and Clark, 2011; Beltman and Schaeben, 2012). Advantages of peer mentoring include helping students make the most of opportunities within the university (Andrews and Clark, 2011). It has been identified that this is an advantage for the mentors as well as the mentees as helping others mentors also become more aware of resources provided by the university (Beltman and Schaeben, 2012). Mentors also identify that they gained personal satisfaction and enjoyment from supporting others and giving something back (Beltman and Schaeben, 2012). This links to one of the five paths to well-being, that of 'giving'. In addition, mentors build networks and develop friendships (Colvin and Ashman, 2010).

Peer mentoring is not without its challenges. These can include personality clashes from unsuitable pairing, lack of skills or confidence, logistical or communication barriers (Andrews and Clark, 2011). There is a need for training and ongoing support for mentors and mentees. A mentorship agreement needs to be drawn up to protect mentors from being put in a vulnerable position through excessive emotional attachment or over-dependency by the mentee (Colvin and Ashman, 2010). A mentorship agreement may also help to alleviate any concerns on the part of the mentee about the reliability of their mentor (Colvin and Ashman, 2010).

A six-year evaluation of a mentoring programme in Australia identified the following factors that you should consider:

- the recruitment and training of mentors;
- scheduling engagement;
- providing information and support for mentors.

(Hall and Jaugietis, 2011)

Reflection

Explore what centrally managed provision is already available in regard to peer mentoring within your institution.
Consider how you can embed peer mentoring within your programme.
Think about how you would organise, recruit, and train mentors.
What mechanism would you use to promote the idea of peer mentoring?
Consider what ongoing support the mentoring scheme may require.

Transitional support

When students move into this new learning environment they find a different academic culture to that in their school or college. They need to develop a new identity as a university student and become familiar with the expectations and academic culture within the institution. At the same time many will have left established networks of friends and family and be learning to cope both practically and socially in this new setting. This can be a particularly worrying time for students. Student Minds provide a guide to students aimed at helping them navigate their journey into higher education (Student Minds, 2021b). This is a useful resource to which you can signpost your students. When students establish a new social network within their university it provides them with a sense of belonging. This is when the student feels accepted, included, and has some connection to their institution. This has long been recognised as playing a vital role in student retention (Thomas, 2012). A sense of belonging is primarily built through social interaction with both academics and peers (Whitten et al., 2020). Many people draw on the seminal work of Tinto (1975, 1987). His retention model indicates the crucial aspects of academic and social integration, and institutional support (Tinto, 1987). Other important aspects of transition include self-efficacy, the student's belief in their abilities, self-regulation, and the ability to develop into autonomous learners (Brooman and Darwent, 2014).

A key action you can take as programme leader is to examine the engagement opportunities throughout your programme. Enabling students to make friends and build relationships with staff and students helps to develop a sense of belonging (Thomas, 2013). Extracurricular activities such as sports teams and societies can also help students to build relationships and develop friendships beyond their immediate cohort. A key piece of literature is the report from 'What works?'. Student retention and success programme (Thomas, 2012). The report draws on the experience of a variety of projects with emphasis on the need to nurture a sense of belonging. Central to their model of student retention and success is the student engagement. A sense of belonging project undertaken at Bangor University confirmed this importance of academic and social engagement (Ahn and Davis, 2020).

This section of the chapter draws on the findings of the report and other literature to discuss how you as a programme leader can have a positive impact on student transition: how you can help students develop supportive peer relationships, have meaningful interactions with staff and students, develop knowledge, confidence, and identity as a learner, and help them have an experience which is relevant to their interests and goals (Thomas, 2013).

Focusing on the role of programme leader, these principles are adapted from the report (Thomas, 2012).

- Interventions should be embedded into your programme with an opt-out rather opt-in approach to ensure that all your students participate and can benefit from them, not just the more motivated students.
- You should be proactive in trying to engage students, rather than just posting an invitation. For example, mention events during class and encourage discussion about becoming involved.
- The relevance of any activities that you provide should be made clear to students as well as any potential benefits to their engagement.
- The timing of activities is important, some may be one-off opportunities whilst others are best extended over a period of time.

- Activities should be collaborative with both other students and members of staff. Peer-led initiative can be very effective.
- It is useful to monitor the engagement of your students and follow up any cases where there are low levels of engagement. This will help identify students who maybe struggling to adjust. Remember that attendance does not always signify engagement.

The transition period can be divided into three parts: pre-entry, induction, and after induction.

Pre-entry

Students can feel unprepared for university, finding the programme and learning style different from what they expected. Before a student starts you should aim to provide the following:

- information about your programme;
- be clear about your expectations and explore the expectations of your students;
- start the process of developing their academic skills;
- help students build supportive relationships;
- start nurturing a sense of belonging.

(Thomas, 2013)

Pre-entry activities particularly where they involve interaction with other candidates, current students and staff can be valuable in both providing information and also starting the process of engagement and belonging. Some universities will arrange pre-course days, to finalise paperwork and have some welcome activities. A lot of the activity recently will have been moved online; depending on the practicalities and opportunities in the future some of these may remain, others will not. However, even using a remote platforms engagement with others should be encouraged as much as possible. The Advance HE published specific guidance on transition in this era of 'new normal' (Morgan, 2020). This reiterates that the process of building and sense of belonging commences before students join your programme. Returning students will also need additional support before they start their year as they may be unsure what to expect in a changing academic environment (Morgan, 2020).

Make yourself familiar with what your institution provides. Interventions vary between universities, some offering one-day attendance, others having a more extended programme. One pre-academic programme undertaken in the Netherlands was a four-day intervention aimed at changing students' perceptions of effective learning, and to increase the sense of belonging (Van Herpen et al., 2020). The intervention had a positive effect on students engaging with both their peers and academics.

Induction

Induction should continue the processes commenced before the student is enrolled on the programme; socialisation, establishing expectations and developing relationships (Thomas, 2013). For this next stage of the process you should encourage active engagement rather than students just being passive recipients of information. Effective induction activities will facilitate the socialisation and forming of friendships, help to clarify the expectations of a learner at university, and start developing relationships with staff. When planning your induction, you should consider the following:

- Have activities with students within your programme.
- Plan activities over an extended period of time
- Help students get to know each other via ice breakers and group work.
- Hold informal activities so that your students can get to know the staff involved with their programme.
- Provide information that is easily accessible so that students can return to this information as required.
- Continue the process of establishing expectations.

(Thomas, 2013)

After induction

Successful transition into university goes beyond the initial one- or two-week period of induction and it is now recognised as a longer process of acclimatisation. Laing et al. (2005) recommend a spiral induction programme running initially over the first six weeks and then being extended throughout the academic year, scheduling relevant activities at key points (Laing et al., 2005). One of the aims of their programme was to identify students who may be at risk, particularly the quiet ones who may leave the institution through non-attendance. Monitoring participation is an important part in the identification of students at risk of exiting the programme early. You should therefore consider how you can continue to facilitate a smooth transition in the months following induction weeks:

- Continue to nurture staff/student relationships.
- Have real world activities that the student sees as relevant to their future.
- Include interactive teaching and learning strategies
- Have clear information, for example around assessment processes
- Encourage peer relationships.
- Foster a sense of belonging.

(Thomas, 2013)

In summary, student transition into university is complex and there is a lack of consistency between institutions (O'Donnell et al., 2016). It is more than

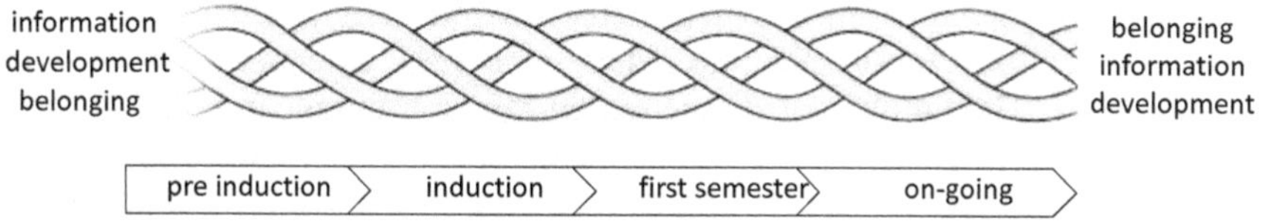

Figure 5.1 The intertwining elements of transition

just a period of time for induction and the delivery of information. It is about social integration and academic engagement (O'Donnell et al., 2016). Figure 5.1 represents the ongoing intertwining elements of **information**, the essential things that students need to know such as assessment regulations, **development**, developing into autonomous learners, and **belonging**, developing connectiveness to the university.

> **Reflection**
> Think about how you currently facilitate a smooth transition and how you might develop this further.
>
> - How early do you start the transition process?
> - How much focus is given to social engagement?
> - How much do you involve other university staff in your induction and transition activities?
> - How do you make your activities relevant to a diverse student population?
> - How and when do you review your transition activities?

Wider issues relating to student experience

Equality, diversity, and inclusion (EDI)

Much of the work around EDI has focused on representation within higher education and it is only relatively recently that focus has turned on the experiences and outcomes, particularly for Black, Asian, and Minority Ethnic students (BAME) and other underrepresented groups including: students from areas of low socioeconomic status, mature students, disabled students, care leavers, carers, refugees, people from Gypsy, Roma, and Traveller communities, children from military families, and people estranged from their families (Office for Students, 2020). Widening participation has made good progress and is important but it is not sufficient in itself to address inequality (Arday and Mirza, 2018; Wong et al. 2021). With the now ethnically diverse student body there is a recognised attainment gap between BAME students and white students (Arday and Mirza, 2018; Tate and Bagguley, 2018). There is indication that a white student is twice as likely to obtain a good degree as a non-white student (Richardson, 2018). Only about half of these can be attributed to the difference in the entry qualification (Richardson, 2018). Thus, we need to examine the experiences of BAME students whilst they are at university. The amount of differences in ethnic attainment varies between programmes and between institutions suggesting that learning teaching and assessment practices impact on this. As a programme leader, it is important to explore the experiences your students particularly if they are experiencing academic failure or exiting from the programme. You should question if this is partly due to the interaction with academics and students (Tate and Bagguley, 2018). It also emphasises the need to be aware of any differences in attainment for your students, particularly patterns over time.

Stereotyping can have damaging psychological effects and erode the self-confidence of students (Mountford-Zimdars et al. 2015). It is not uncommon for female Muslim students to be stereotyped as a passive or oppressed and women wearing the hijab being subjected to well-meaning hyper-surveillance (Mirza and Meetoo, 2018). This disjunction between the Western perception and self-perception can have a negative impact on the student's sense of belonging. Ash et al. (2020) talk about the deficit thinking where educators label students which results in shifting the blame for poor achievement and so on from the institution onto the student. Following the Counter Terrorism and Security Act 2015 there is a statutory duty to inform on students considered vulnerable to radicalisation. There is evidence that some students can experience Islamophobia and increased scrutiny (Durodie, 2016). Incidence of Islamophobia are likely to be go unreported by many students who do not wish to come under further scrutiny, labelled as being over-sensitive, or standout (Saeed, 2018). Up to two-thirds of racial discriminatory incidents go unreported (Wong et al., 2021). Students are either unaware of or lack confidence in university welfare services (Saeed, 2018).

Despite claims that we are now in a post-racial era, institutional racism still exists (Wong et al., 2021). This can be seen within higher education with predominately white senior managers and programmes with white curricula, despite strategies aimed at promoting race equality such as the Race Equality Charter Mark (Tate and Bagguley, 2016; Bhopal and Henderson, 2021). Institutions often focus on support resources for BAME students and intolerance training for staff (Ash et al., 2020). But institutional policies alone cannot promote anti-racism. Racism has been around for centuries and many forms remain invisible and unacknowledged (Ash et al,. 2020). Addressing overt racist acts is essential but does not address deeply rooted systemic racism (Ash et al., 2020). This section of the book cannot explore the complexities of racism but looks at what you can do as a programme leader to strive towards an anti-racist programme. Mirza (2018) discusses some of the ways in which academics address issues and support BAME students. Recognising students base decisions on the sense of who they are and their place in the world, sticking to what they know is achievable and culturally comfortable (Mirza, 2018). They learn to navigate their journey through higher education, giving up parts of themselves along the way in order to belong (Mirza, 2018). Negative attitudes towards against students can threaten their sense of belonging and academic performance (Wong et al., 2021). Mirza (2018) concluded that academics lack confidence and receive limited training and support around issues of multiculturalism and inclusive pedagogy and practice. It was also recognised that talking about ethnic and religious differences in classroom discussions is avoided (Tate and Bagguley, 2016; Mirza, 2018). Conversations about race and racism may be difficult but they help students, both BAME and white, to develop critical thinking around anti-oppression and anti-racism (Tate and Bagguley, 2016).

Equal opportunity is not just about treating everybody the same. If this approach is taken then it may leave struggling students in need of additional support at a disadvantage (Mirza, 2018). However, whilst providing support resources for BAME students is important it does not offer a permanent solution to systemic racism (Ash et al. 2020). Students accept moderate racist behaviour and micro-aggression such as jokes or comments on accents as normal (Wong et al., 2021). When students tolerate or dismiss forms of racism as poor humour or misunderstanding it can lead to disempowerment, perpetuating the racial inequalities (Wong et al., 2021).

Decolonising the curricular is the buzzword currently banded about but what does this actually mean? How do we decolonise this whiteness and white supremacy? Much of the literature around decolonisation stems from South Africa; it is multi-layered and complex. Decolonisation is more than just about changing the content of the curricula or the reading list; it is also about how the content is delivered, attitudes, and beliefs (Vandeyar, 2020). The first crucial aspect is to view others as different and not inferior (Tate and Bagguley, 2017). We need to recognise our own identity and that of our institution (Tate and Bagguley, 2017). To do this we need to reflect on the world we are situated in (Bhambra et al., 2018). It is said that people outside of the BAME community can be unaware or blind to how they might be perpetuating whiteness (Wong et al., 2021). Much of the pressure to decolonise the curriculum is student led (Pimblott, 2020). The UK campaign 'Why is my curriculum white?' seeks to challenge the lack of diversity in curricula and clearly highlights that there is work to be done as a programme leader to examine your programme through the lens of the decolonisation (Bhambra et al., 2018). Part of the decolonise movement is calling for the recognition of alternative knowledge and eroding the traditional academia (Pimblott, 2020). Decolonisation is about reconstructing the way we think and although there are structural and organisational aspects to decolonisation it is the responsibility of every individual to think constructively about it (Mpungose, 2020). When examining you may find that your programme, including student demographics, curricular design and content are Eurocentric (Bhambra et al., 2018). One focus of decolonisation is the diversifying of reading lists (Bird and Pitman, 2020). To be successful we need to move past token diversity to thoroughly transform the knowledge base (Pimblott, 2020).

Strategies that you can use as programme leader to promote anti-racism include:

- Provide a safe space for opened dialogue both for academic staff delivering on your programme and students.
- Acknowledge the existence of racism and make all students aware that racism does exist and the forms it could take from explicit to implicit.
- Work with BAME students to identify and address any issues around reporting incidents of racism.
- Ensure that information and policies about EDI are readily available and well publicised.
- Make it clear what welfare facilities are available and how to access these.
- Reflect on and challenge the diversity in your curriculum through the lens of decolonisation.
- Engage with a range of stakeholders to have a transparent, frank discussion about the contents of your reading list.

Using analytics to support student experience

There is increasing interest in a learning analytics. Students leave a data footprint throughout their interaction at university which can help us gain an understanding about their experience (Shacklock, 2016). These can be a valuable asset to programme leaders. Sclater (2014) explored how learning analytics were used across different higher and further education institutions. A further review of UK and international practice was undertaken in 2016 (Sclater et al., 2016). These reports provide case studies of how analytics can be used. Many institutions use analytics as a mode of enhancing the student learning experience. Data can be gathered from a wide variety of sources such as attendance monitoring via swipe cards. At an institutional level learning analytics can be used to ensure funding is evidence based and used effectively; for example, monitoring the use of computers in the library.

Learner analytics can contribute to:

- quality assurance and quality improvement by providing data that can lead to improved practice;
- improving retention rates by identifying at risk students;
- equality within the programme, for example by identifying any attainment gaps between populations;
- enabling a personalised approach to delivery by providing a greater understanding of engagement within the programme.

(Sclater et al., 2016)

As a programme leader, is very useful to learn how to effectively use learning analytics. Some institutions may have a central data source; if not it is useful to gather all of your data and keep it in one place with an effective filing system so that data can be easily retrieved. Check that your data is accurate and up-to-date because programme leaders are frequently asked for the same information from different people. This is where spending time gathering and organising your data will save time in the long run because it will be easily accessed rather than you spending time looking for and regathering information.

Learner analytics can be used as a tool for quality assurance and quality improvement by identifying any issues with modules within your programme; for example, any delay in providing feedback. It can be used to identify student engagement by monitoring attendance with a virtual learning environment. It can be used to identify at risk students either individually or subgroups such as mature students. Having a better understanding of your student population can help to reduce attrition by early identification of potential issues such as lack of engagement. You may also choose to have student-facing analytics. Allowing students to have information about how they are progressing and engaging with the programme may motivate students or prompt them to seek further support.

Vignette

As a programme leader I have used learner analytics to both identify students who may need additional support and to encourage student attendance.

Face-to-face attendance of my students was monitored via registers at each session. The data from these was collated via administrators and provided on a monthly basis. Using this information students were contacted via email if they had missed a small number of sessions and invited to a meeting with myself as programme leader if a large number of sessions had been missed. Students generally responded by explaining the reasons for their absence and remedial action could be taken to address any issues identified. Monitoring attendance and contacting students in cases of absence also promoted that the students were seen as individuals and would be missed.

Engagement with the virtual learning environment can also be monitored with some systems. You can see when students have last accessed learning materials and engaged in interactive platforms such as discussion boards. This is not only allowing you to see what material is been accessed most frequently; it also allows you to identify students who are not engaging as proactively with the programme as others. I have found it valuable to contact these students and identify if there are any issues inhibiting their study. This helps to increase the students' sense of belonging and the feeling that we care for them as individual students.

Summary

The mental health of students in higher education is high on the agenda across the world and is something that should be considered by programme leaders who have an important role in the mental well-being of their students. Your programme should be challenging and at times may be stressful for your students. You can create an environment that is inclusive, caring, compassionate, and supportive. There are ways of embedding mental well-being into your curriculum and creating conditions that facilitate positive mental health by being active, learning, taking notice, connecting, and giving. Personal tutoring can impact on student experience and retention. There are ways that you can support this within your programme, ensuring each student can be signposted to the support they need. Supportive peer relationships such as peer mentoring and peer tutoring provide mechanisms for supporting your students and help develop employability skills. The organisation of these initiatives such as the recruitment and training of mentors and peer tutors is something for you to consider. These can particularly help the transition into university and onto your programme. There is now an ethnically diverse body of students entering higher education, bringing issues of equality, diversity, and inclusion into the role of a programme leader. In this digital era, students leave a data footprint throughout their interaction at university which can help you gain an understanding of your students' experience and be an asset in your role as programme leader.

References

Ahn, M.Y. and Davis, H.H., 2020. Four domains of students' sense of belonging to university. *Studies in Higher Education*, 45(3), pp. 622–634.

Andrews, J. and Clark, R., 2011. *Peer mentoring works!* Available from http://publications.aston.ac.uk/id/eprint/17968/ (accessed 2 December 2021).

Arday, J. and Mirza, H.S. (eds), 2018. *Dismantling race in higher education: Racism, whiteness and decolonising the academy.* Springer.

Ash, A.N., Hill, R., Risdon, S., and Jun, A., 2020. Anti-racism in higher education: A model for change. *Race and Pedagogy Journal: Teaching and Learning for Justice*, 4(3), p. 2.

Bain, P., Wareing, A., and Henderson, I., 2017. A review of peer-assisted learning to deliver interprofessional supplementary image interpretation skills. *Radiography*, 23, pp. S64–S69.

Beltman, S. and Schaeben, M., 2012. Institution-wide peer mentoring: Benefits for mentors. *The International Journal of the First Year in Higher Education*, 3(2), pp. 33–44.

Bene, K.L. and Bergus, G., 2014. When learners become teachers. *Family Medicine*, 46, pp. 783–787.

Bhambra, G.K., Gebrial, D., and Nişancıoğlu, K., 2018. *Decolonising the university.* Pluto Press.

Bhopal, K. and Henderson, H., 2021. Competing inequalities: gender versus race in higher education institutions in the UK. *Educational Review*, 73(2), pp. 153–169.

Bird, K.S. and Pitman, L., 2020. How diverse is your reading list? Exploring issues of representation and decolonisation in the UK. *Higher Education*, 79(5), pp. 903–920.

Braine, M.E. and Parnell, J., 2011. *Exploring students' perceptions and experience of personal tutors. Nurse Education Today*, 31(8), pp. 904–910.

Broglia, E., Millings, A., and Barkham, M., 2018. Challenges to addressing student mental health in embedded counselling services: A survey of UK higher and further education institutions. *British Journal of Guidance & Counselling*, 46(4), pp. 441–455.

Brooman, S. and Darwent, S., 2014. Measuring the beginning: A quantitative study of the transition to higher education. *Studies in Higher Education*, 39(9), pp. 1523–1541.

Bush, M., 2011. Mindfulness in higher education. *Contemporary Buddhism*, 12(1), pp. 183–197.

Chirikov, I., Soria, K.M., Horgos, B., and Jones-White, D., 2020. Undergraduate and graduate students' mental health during the COVID-19 pandemic. *UC Berkeley SERU Consortium Reports pages 1 to 10*. Available from https://escholarship.org/uc/item/80k5d5hw (accessed 12 April 2022)

Clarke, A.J., Burgess, A., van Diggele, C., and Mellis, C., 2019. The role of reverse mentoring in medical education: Current insights. *Advances in Medical Education and Practice*, 10, pp. 693–701.

Clegg, S. and Bufton, S., 2008. Student support through personal development planning: Retrospection and time. *Research Papers in Education*, 23(4), pp. 435–450.

Collings, R., Swanson, V., and Watkins, R., 2014. The impact of peer mentoring on levels of student well-being, integration and retention: A controlled comparative evaluation of residential students in UK higher education. *Higher Education*, 68(6), pp. 927–942.

Colvin, J.W. and Ashman, M., 2010. Roles, risks, and benefits of peer mentoring relationships in higher education. *Mentoring & Tutoring: Partnership in Learning*, 18(2), pp. 121–134.

Cottrell, S., 2015. *Skills for success: Personal development and employability*. Macmillan International Higher Education.

Deasy, C., Coughlan, B., Pironom, J., Jourdan, D., and Mannix-McNamara, P., 2014. Psychological distress and coping amongst higher education students: A mixed method enquiry. *Plos One*, 9(12), p. e115193.

Dobinson-Harrington, A., 2006. Personal tutor encounters: Understanding the experience. *Nursing Standard (through 2013)*, 20(50), pp. 35–42.

Durodie, B., 2016. *Securitising education to prevent terrorism or losing direction?British Journal of Educational Studies*, 64(1), pp. 21–35.

Elshami, W., Abuzaid, M., and Abdalla, M.E., 2020. Radiography students' perceptions of peer assisted learning. *Radiography*, 26(2), pp. e109–e113.

Ergas, O. and Hadar, L.L., 2021. Does mindfulness belong in higher education? An eight year research of students' experiences. *Pedagogy, Culture & Society*, pp. 1–19. DOI: doi:10.1080/14681366.2021.1906307.

Field, M., Burke, J.M., McAllister, D., and Lloyd, D.M., 2007. Peer-assisted learning: A novel approach to clinical skills learning for medical students. *Medical education*, 41(4), pp. 411–418.

Gidman, J., 2001. The role of the personal tutor: A literature review. *Nurse Education Today*, 21(5), pp. 359–365.

Hagenauer, G. and Volet, S.E., 2014. *Teacher–student relationship at university: An important yet under-researched field. Oxford Review of Education*, 40(3), pp. 370–388.

Hall, R. and Jaugietis, Z., 2011. Developing peer mentoring through evaluation. *Innovative Higher Education*, 36(1), pp. 41–52.

Hamilton, J., Stevens, G., and Girdler, S., 2016. Becoming a mentor: The impact of training and the experience of mentoring university students on the autism spectrum. *PLoS one*, 11(4), p. e0153204.

Hewitt, R., 2019. Measuring well-being in higher education. *HEPI Policy Note 13*. Higher Education Policy Institute.

Houghton, A.M. and Anderson, J., 2017. Embedding mental well-being in the curriculum: maximising success in higher education. *Higher Education Academy*, 68. http s://www.advance-he.ac.uk/knowledge-hub/embedding-mental-wellbeing-curriculum-maximising-success-higher-education (accessed 12 April 2022)

Jelfs, A., Richardson, J.T., and Price, L., 2009. Student and tutor perceptions of effective tutoring in distance education. *Distance Education*, 30(3), pp. 419–441.

Khalid, H., Shahid, S., Punjabi, N., and Sahdev, N., 2018. An integrated 2-year clinical skills peer tutoring scheme in a UK-based medical school: Perceptions of tutees and peer tutors. *Advances in Medical Education and Practice*, 9, p. 423.

Kenney, S. and Grim, M., 2015. Development and implementation of a curriculum infusion plan for alcohol abuse education in a college population. *American Journal of Health Education*, 46(1), pp. 24–32.

Laidlaw, A., McLellan, J., and Ozakinci, G., 2016. Understanding undergraduate student perceptions of mental health, mental well-being and help-seeking behaviour. *Studies in Higher Education*, 41(12), pp. 2156–2168.

Laing, C., Robinson, A., and Johnston, V., 2005. Managing the transition into higher education: An on-line spiral induction programme. *Active Learning in Higher Education*, 6(3), pp. 243–255.

Luck, C., 2010. Challenges faced by tutors in higher education. *Psychodynamic Practice*, 16(3), pp. 273–287.

Martin, J.M., 2010. Stigma and student mental health in higher education. *Higher Education Research & Development*, 29(3), pp. 259–274.

McFarlane, K.J., 2016. Tutoring the tutors: Supporting effective personal tutoring. *Active Learning in Higher Education*, 17(1), pp. 77–88.

Meertens, R., 2016. Utilisation of a peer assisted learning scheme in an undergraduate diagnostic radiography module. *Radiography*, 22(1), pp. e69–e74.

MIND, 2021. What is the Mentally Healthy Universities Programme? Available from https://www.mind.org.uk/information-support/tips-for-everyday-living/student-life/#MentallyHealthyUniversitiesProgramme (accessed 22 October 2021).

Mirza, H.S., 2018. Black bodies 'out of place' in academic spaces: Gender, race, faith and culture in post-race times. In J. Arday and H. Safia Mirza (eds), *Dismantling Race in Higher Education* (pp. 175–193). Palgrave Macmillan.

Mirza, H.S. and Meetoo, V., 2018. Empowering Muslim girls? Post-feminism, multiculturalism and the production of the 'model' Muslim female student in British schools. *British Journal of Sociology of Education*, 39(2), pp. 227–241.

Morgan, M., 2020. An exceptional transition to higher education: Induction of new and returning students during the 'new normal' year. Advance HE. Available from https://www.advance-he.ac.uk/knowledge-hub/exceptional-transition-higher-education-induction-new-and-returning-students-during (accessed 23 October 2021).

Mountford-Zimdars, A.K., Sanders, J., Jones, S., Sabri, D., and Moore, J., 2015. Causes of differences in student outcomes. Higher Education Funding Council for England.

Mpungose, C.B., 2020. Is Moodle a platform to decolonise the university curriculum? Lecturers' reflections. *Africa Education Review*, 17(1), pp. 100–115.

National Union of Students, 2015. NUS Charter on Personal Tutors. Available from https://www.nusconnect.org.uk/resources/nus-charter-on-personal-tutors (accessed 22 October 2021).

Neville, L., 2007. *The personal tutor's handbook*. Macmillan International Higher Education.

O'Donnell, V.L., Kean, M., and Stevens, G., 2016. Student transition in higher education. Higher Education Academy. Available from https://www.heacademy. ac.uk/system/files/downloads/student_transition_in_higher_education.pdf.

Office for National Statistics, 2018. Estimated suicide among higher education students, England and Wales: Experimental Statistics. Available from https://www.ons.gov.uk/peoplepopulationandcommunity/birthsdeathsandmarriages/deaths/articles/estimatingsuicideamonghighereducationstudentsenglandandwalesexperimentalstatistics/2018-06-25 (accessed 22 October 2021).

Office for National Statistics, 2021. Suicides in England and Wales: 2020 registrations. Available from https://www.ons.gov.uk/peoplepopulationandcommunity/birthsdeathsandmarriages/deaths/bulletins/suicidesintheunitedkingdom/2020registrations#suicide-patterns-by-age (accessed 25 November 2021).

Office for Students, 2020. Access and participation glossary. Available from https://www.officeforstudents.org.uk/advice-and-guidance/promoting-equal-opportunities/access-and-participation-glossary/ (accessed 25 November 2021).

Office for Students, 2021. Student mental health. Available from https://www.officeforstudents.org.uk/advice-and-guidance/student-wellbeing-and-protection/student-mental-health/resources-and-case-studies-for-higher-education-providers/ (accessed 22 October 2021).

Parker, P., Kram, K.E., and Hall, D.T., 2013. Exploring risk factors in peer coaching: A multilevel approach. *The journal of applied behavioral science*, 49(3), pp. 361–387.

Pimblott, K., 2020. Decolonising the university: The origins and meaning of a movement. *The Political Quarterly*, 91(1), pp. 210–216.

Reavley, N. and Jorm, A.F., 2010. Prevention and early intervention to improve mental health in higher education students: a review. *Early Intervention in Psychiatry*, 4(2), pp. 132–142.

Reidlinger, D.P., Lawrence, J., Thomas, J.E., and Whelan, K., 2017. Peer-assisted learning and small-group teaching to improve practice placement quality and capacity in dietetics. *Nutrition & Dietetics*, 74(4), pp. 349–356.

Richardson, J.T., 2018. Understanding the under-attainment of ethnic minority students in UK higher education: The known knowns and the known unknowns. In *Dismantling Race in Higher Education* (pp. 87–102). Palgrave Macmillan.

Rückert, H.W., 2015. *Students' mental health and psychological counselling in Europe. Mental Health & Prevention*, 3(1–2), pp. 34–40.

Saeed, T., 2018. Islamophobia in higher education: Muslim students and the "duty of care". In *Dismantling Race in Higher Education* (pp. 233–250). Palgrave Macmillan.

Sahu, P., 2020. Closure of universities due to coronavirus disease 2019 (COVID-19): impact on education and mental health of students and academic staff. *Cureus*, 12 (4). DOI: doi:10.7759/cureus.7541.

Sarmento, M., 2015. A "mental health profile" of higher education students. *Procedia-Social and Behavioral Sciences*, 191, pp. 12–20.

Saunders, D., 1992. Peer tutoring in higher education. *Studies in Higher Education*, 17 (2), pp. 211–218.

Schreiber, B., 2018. Mental health at universities: Universities are not in loco parentis–Students are active partners in mental health. *Journal of Student Affairs in Africa*, 6 (2), pp. 121–127.

Schwind, J.K., McCay, E., Beanlands, H., Martin, L.S., Martin, J., and Binder, M., 2017. Mindfulness practice as a teaching–learning strategy in higher education: A qualitative exploratory pilot study. *Nurse education today*, 50, pp. 92–96.

Sclater, N., 2014. Learning analytics: The current state of play in UK higher and further education, Jisc. Available from https://repository.jisc.ac.uk/5657/1/Learning_analytics_report.pdf (accessed 23 October 2021).

Sclater, N., Peasgood, A., and Mullan, J., 2016. Learning analytics in higher education. Jisc. https://www.jisc.ac.uk/reports/learning-analytics-in-higher-education (accessed 8 February 2017).

Secomb, J., 2008. A systematic review of peer teaching and learning in clinical education. *Journal of Clinical Nursing*, 17(6), pp. 703–716.

Shacklock, X., 2016. *From bricks to clicks: The potential of data and analytics in higher education*. Higher Education Commission.

Siew, C.T., Mazzucchelli, T.G., Rooney, R., and Girdler, S., 2017. A specialist peer mentoring program for university students on the autism spectrum: A pilot study. *PloS one*, 12(7), p. e0180854.

Stephen, D.E., O'Connell, P., and Hall, M., 2008. 'Going the extra mile', 'fire-fighting', or laissez-faire? Re-evaluating personal tutoring relationships within mass higher education. *Teaching in Higher Education*, 13(4), pp. 449–460.

Stevenson, N., 2009. Enhancing the student experience by embedding personal tutoring in the curriculum. *Journal of Hospitality, Leisure, Sports and Tourism Education (Pre-2012)*, 8(2), pp. 117–122.

Student Minds, 2021a. Support for a friend. Available from https://www.studentminds.org.uk/supportforafriend.html (accessed 22 October 2021).

Student Minds, 2021b. Transition into university. Available from https://www.studentminds.org.uk/transitionintouniversity.html (accessed 22 October 2021).

Tai, J., Molloy, E., Haines, T., and Canny, B., 2016. Same-level peer-assisted learning in medical clinical placements: A narrative systematic review. *Medical Education*, 50 (4), pp. 469–484.

Tate, S.A. and Bagguley, P., 2017. Building the anti-racist university: Next steps. *Race Ethnicity and Education*, 20(3), pp. 289299.

Tate, S.A. and Bagguley, P. (eds), 2018. *Building the anti-racist university*. Routledge.

The Wellbeing Thesis, 2021. Available from https://thewellbeingthesis.org.uk/ (accessed 22 October 2021).

Thomas, L., 2012. *Building student engagement and belonging in higher education at a time of change*. Paul Hamlyn Foundation, 100, pp. 1–99.

Thomas, L., 2013. What works? Facilitating an effective transition into higher education. *Widening Participation and Lifelong Learning*, 14(1), pp. 4–24.

Tinto, V., 1975. Dropout from higher education: A theoretical synthesis of recent research. *Review of Educational Research*, 45(1), pp. 89–125.

Tinto, V., 1987. *Leaving college: Rethinking the causes and cures of student attrition*. University of Chicago Press.

Topping, K.J., 1996. The effectiveness of peer tutoring in further and higher education: A typology and review of the literature. *Higher Education*, 32(3), pp. 321–345.

Vandeyar, S., 2020. Why decolonising the South African university curriculum will fail. *Teaching in Higher Education*, 25(7), pp. 783–796.

Van Herpen, S.G., Meeuwisse, M., Hofman, W.A., and Severiens, S.E., 2020. A head start in higher education: The effect of a transition intervention on interaction, sense of belonging, and academic performance. *Studies in Higher Education*, 45(4), pp. 862–877.

Vickers, M., McCarthy, F., and Zammit, K., 2017. Peer mentoring and intercultural understanding: Support for refugee-background and immigrant students beginning university study. *International Journal of Intercultural Relations*, 60, pp. 198–209.

Wagner, L., 1982. *Peer teaching: Historical perspectives* (Vol. 5). Praeger.

Whitten, D., James, A., and Roberts, C., 2020. Factors that contribute to a sense of belonging in business students on a small 4-year public commuter campus in the Midwest. *Journal of College Student Retention: Research, Theory & Practice*, 22(1), pp. 99–117.

Wong, B., Elmorally, R., Copsey-Blake, M., Highwood, E., and Singarayer, J., 2021. Is race still relevant? Student perceptions and experiences of racism in higher education. *Cambridge Journal of Education*, 51(3), pp. 359–375.

Young, J.R., Bullough, Jr, R.V., Draper, R.J., Smith, L.K., and Erickson, L.B., 2005. Novice teacher growth and personal models of mentoring: Choosing compassion over inquiry. *Mentoring & Tutoring: Partnership in Learning*, 13(2), pp. 169–188.

6 Involving external expertise

External expertise

External expertise is one of the themes of the advice and guidance related to the QAA Quality Code (QAA, 2018a). External experts are not directly involved with a programme, but can input into all aspects such as design, delivery, assessment, and evaluation (QAA, 2018b). These experts can include: external examiners, advisers, such as from professional, statutory, and regulatory bodies (PRSB), employers, placement providers, guest speakers, students, and alumni. This chapter will focus on people who are invited to contribute across the life cycle of the student, such as guest lecturers, representatives from PRSBs, work placements, alumni, or employers. Particularly for programmes related to health and social care, external expertise is also drawn from people who have recent personal experience of using or caring for someone using health or social care services. These are known as experts-by-experience or service users and carers. Their involvement is driven by patient advocacy groups and is increasingly included in policy and guidance from governing and professional bodies. There are several reasons for including experts-by-experience, such as demands from the service users, to increase the power and control of service users, and to challenge entrenched professional attitudes (Lathlean et al., 2006). There are other terms used mostly in connection with research, business–university collaboration (Dowling, 2015), and university–industry collaboration (Ankrah and Al-Tabbaa, 2015; Awasthy et al., 2020). There is a drive to improve the breadth and range of connections between universities and industry (Dowling, 2015). The review by Ankrah and Al-Tabbaa (2015) recognised that there are different forms of relationships between universities and industry. These start at programme level. Links with industry will help develop work-ready students and increase the potential for collaboration, particularly in terms of student projects being aligned with the requirements of industry, leading to real-world application of their research (Awasthy, et al., 2020). Relationships with industry will help students become more entrepreneurial (Morisson and Pattinson, 2020). When integrated effectively they can drive forward democracy and transparency in education.

DOI: 10.4324/9781003126355-7

Integrating external expertise throughout your programme should overall enhance the student experience. Using interviews to explore the cooperation between universities and employers in Europe, Rakovska, Pavin, and Melink (2014) found there to be a gap between education and industry. Collaboration can reduce this gap and increase the quality and relevance of the practical training and curriculum. To ensure that students undertake learning that is relevant to the workplace and future employment, programme leaders have a role in building university–industry collaboration. This can be done by engaging with external expertise.

Benefits to the student include:

- the development of transferable employability skills;
- the acquisition of entrepreneurial awareness;
- developing a greater understanding of the application of theory to practice;
- encouraging students to adopt a personhood approach to their practice;
- engaging with activity within a programme can also benefit the external expert;
- it can develop their confidence and employability skills;
- providing a platform for sharing personal experiences;
- gaining satisfaction from contributing to the development of others;
- they can learn from interaction with students;
- it can contribute to their continual professional development.

Organising external expert involvement

Organisational and administrative issues can present barriers to the involvement of external expertise. Some institutions may involve external experts as a tick-box exercise to fulfil governing body requirements. This should be avoided to ensure that higher education benefits fully from involving external expertise. Thus, there needs to be a robust infrastructure to support the involvement of external experts and prevent it from being tokenistic, only used to fulfil requirements rather than a meaningful experience. Often their involvement is reliant on one or two enthusiastic individuals, therefore structures need to be in place to support a culture of inclusion and move towards a partnership between university and industry.

To support the engagement of external expertise within your programme you should ensure the following are in place:

- Information, training, and assistance to the external expert are available.
- The specific role required by the external expert is clear and that they can meet the responsibilities within that role.
- Ensure the skills of the external expert match the needs of the programme.
- Have one main point of contact for any questions or concerns that the external expert may have about engaging with the programme.

- Have a mechanism for and be receptive to any comment from the external expert regarding ways in which tasks might be accomplished.
- Ensure the external expert understands the appropriate standards of performance expected and encourages and supports them to achieve and maintain them.
- A commitment to promoting equal opportunities and preventing discrimination for all, and be willing to provide equal access, where appropriate, to facilities and opportunities.
- Ensure confidentiality about any personal information the external expert may provide is maintained.
- A system of reward and recognition.

Reflection
It is useful to look at some overarching questions about the engagement of external expertise in higher education. Think about these in relation to your programme:

- What inhibits engagement?
- What is good practice?
- What is the rationale for the engagement?

Identifying, recruiting, and rewarding the experts

Involving external experts requires identifying appropriate individuals. This can be problematic, and often results in external experts being identified and recruited through connections within the university. There may be external experts already engaging within your university and it could be possible for staff members to put you in contact with these individuals. Other ways of identifying appropriate people are through charities and organisations, or the role could be advertised. Your normal university policies and processes should be followed when recruiting external experts to ensure equality and diversity are considered.

There will be cost implications when involving external experts within your programme. These need to be factored in when budgeting. Universities need to be flexible in the way they reward and recognise the contribution of external experts. For some receiving payment may affect their other sources of income, particularly if they are on benefits. Reward and recognition are not always about money – there are other forms of recognition:

- The external expert should always be thanked for their contribution both formally and informally.
- They should be offered feedback on their engagement.
- It may be appropriate to share programme evaluations with those who have contributed to the programme.
- There may be some personal development opportunities that the university can offer external experts.

- External experts are able to use their experiences in CVs and job applications.
- It may be possible to invite external experts to the graduation ceremony.

Facilitating engagement

Once identified you should build good relationships with your external experts as this will help to facilitate effective engagement. You should ensure clarity around what is expected of them and acknowledge potential power imbalances between external experts and academic staff. It is good to have a clear statement around the ethos of engaging external expertise. This can also help to tackle some of the practical barriers that you may come across. Particularly for health and social care programmes you should be mindful of the physical and emotional burden on the individual. During their engagement, external experts may divulge personal, sensitive information. Students and staff members are expected to respect that information and to ensure it is kept private and that confidentiality is observed at all times. If you provide effective support you are more likely to achieve sustainable engagement and provide an effective learning experience. Good support requires planning and preparation. You should be in contact with the external expert and assess what they need.

Some things to consider are:

- help with the preparation of delivery materials;
- transport;
- parking permits;
- finding teaching/meeting rooms.

Following any engagement debriefing should take place with the external expert. This should be both to provide them with feedback on their engagement and to receive feedback from them. External experts have the right to complain, raise concerns, and comment on their engagement activities. Any problems, grievances, and difficulties which may be encountered while engaging with the university should be dealt with promptly. If the external experts have been engaged in face-to-face activity with students, targeted feedback from students is encouraged to inform future activities.

Engaging with experts takes planning and organisation. This can be broken down into actions to take before, during, and after engagement. The planning needs to include aspects relating to the external experts, students, and the academic.

These apply to all engagement. The following sections explore engagement during different aspects of the life cycle of the student from admission to assessment.

Table 6.1 Actions to consider

	Before	*During*	*After*
External expert	Before undertaking any activity, the expert should be provided with a description of their role and a point of contact if this needs clarifying.	Some experts may have competence and confidence in engaging with students or other activities you have invited them to do, but it is good practice for a member of staff to remain present.	There should be a platform for providing feedback on their experience as an external expert. There may be some paperwork to complete for payment, etc.
Students	Students should be briefed about what to expect from a session delivered by an external expert.	Students should behave respectfully toward the external expert.	Students should have the opportunity to provide feedback on their session involving an external expert.
Academic staff	The academic should identify an appropriate external expert and provide a clear remit of what is required from the external expert.	It is good practice for an academic to remain with the external expert throughout their engagement with students.	Seek feedback from both the students and external experts. Follow any process for reward and recognition of work undertaken by the external expert.

External experts involved in the admissions process

Using the example of healthcare education, there is a requirement for values-based recruitment which is an approach that is used to ensure students have values and behaviours that align with the values of the NHS constitution (Health Education England, 2021). There is a national values-based recruitment framework that sets out core requirements that universities are expected to embed into their recruitment process. One of the methods advised, multiple mini-interviews, lends itself to having external experts directly involved in these interviews, as well as representatives from placement providers. Over the last couple of years, most recruitment activity has moved online, making it more challenging to provide direct involvement of external experts in the recruitment of students. However, involving external expertise in some way is still valuable for university programmes. One way to do this is to have external experts involved in the development of the recruitment activity. At present this is likely to be in the development of interview questions. For many programmes, the selection is only via the written application. If this is the case then external experts could be involved in developing the selection criteria and what we are looking for in a personal statement that makes a candidate suitable for a programme.

Service users and carers have been involved in the recruitment of health and social care, and psychology students with positive experiences and some challenges (Matka et al., 2009; Rhodes and Nyawata, 2011). They can offer a unique perspective on the attitudes and abilities of candidates. It also sends a clear message at first contact with the university about the importance of clients (Matka et al., 2009). However, service users may have personal reasons for being involved and this may result in a lack of impartiality. This emphasises the need for external experts to be adequately prepared for any role they undertake. Similarly, any academics involved in the process may have concerns about working with external experts and what to do if there is a disparity in the outcome for a candidate. However, the external experts tend to agree with the academic's opinion in the qualities they were looking for, and that disagreements were rare (Matka et al., 2009; Rhodes and Nyawata, 2011).

Vignette

As programme leader, I was keen to integrate expert-by-experience involvement throughout my programme. This was a requirement of the Health and Care Professions Council validation but I did not want to engage in this as a tick-box exercise. I believed that it would enhance the programme and the student experience. One of the first things was for them to be involved in the recruitment of students. As student recruitment at the time was via multiple mini stations, I thought they could easily take part in these. It may have been the choice of the external expert or inadequate briefing that led to clashes about whether a candidate should be selected or not due to the length of their skirt. This was resolved through a discussion but this incident and other logistical challenges of finding service users for every recruitment event resulted in taking a different approach the following year and rather than having service users present at the recruitment events I worked with them on developing a patient-centred task for the candidates to complete.

Reflection

Why and how might you involve external experts in the recruitment of students onto your programme?

External expertise involved in curriculum delivery

Involving external experts in the delivery of programmes is highly valuable. A large multicentre qualitative study looking at external experts' integration in the training of mental health nursing found that it bridged the theory–practice gap and that the unique perspectives brought by the external experts provided a valuable learning experience (Happell et al., 2020). The inclusion of external experts is not unique to health and social care. Sánchez et al. (2019) highlight the need for computing students to see the value of establishing relationships with clients and engaged experts from the profession to take part in seminars with students. In their evaluation they found is that experts provided a genuine and valuable point of view (Sánchez et al., 2019). There are many ways in which external experts can be involved in the delivery of the curriculum.

- Role-playing can a valuable exercise in which external experts can take on the role of customer or consumer in a particular situation in which the student can learn.
- External experts can provide feedback to students for example if they had observed the students in a simulation exercise or from actual placement experience.
- With the facilitation of an academic, external experts can be involved in teaching in a classroom environment. They can present their unique experience and answer questions from students.
- It may not always be practical to have an external expert physically involved in the delivery of the curriculum. However, it may be feasible for them to be involved in the development of material for delivery by an academic. This could be didactic material or the development of scenarios for problem-based learning.
- A cost-effective way of involvement is recording external experts as a talking head or as an interview. This then allows the material to be used by different cohorts of students.
- Online discussion forums can be a valuable source of information about any particular group of people. Similarly, you may be able to engage an external expert to give feedback to students and be involved in student discussion boards.

Whichever way you decide to incorporate external experts it is important to match the skills and abilities of the expert with the intended activity. You should also ensure they are well prepared and briefed so that they deliver what is expected. Students also need to prepare. As a programme leader, you should be fostering a culture that promotes respect for each other and value individual differences. This means that you will not condone, tolerate, or ignore any form of discrimination or unacceptable behaviour. It is therefore important that students are briefed on what they can expect to experience during engagement with the external expert and on what is expected regarding their behaviour. There may be specific ways students should interact with the visiting expert. After any engagement, the student should have a platform on which to provide feedback. This is both valuable to you as an academic in future planning and the external expert will benefit from student feedback.

Vignette
I have had mixed success with involving service users in the delivery of my programme. Some have been very enriching experiences for the students; occasionally they have had a negative impact on some students. One time I arranged for a service user to come and talk about their condition and treatment. As he had been in to talk to students in previous years, he took the session without an academic present. Some students complained that he was too graphic. Perhaps he had become a 'professional service users' and was aiming to shock the students. The lessons I learnt from this were two-fold. One is that all service users should be accompanied by an academic. Whilst service users are experts in their experience, they are not usually trained in classroom management. The other is to consider the lifespan of the service user and at what point they are too removed from their experience. This will depend on what you would like them to talk about. I arranged some sessions with a group of people with learning disabilities that evaluated well year after year. These were facilitated by an academic.

Reflection
Think about where and how you might involve external experts in the delivery of your programme.

External expertise involved in student assessment

External experts may be involved in the assessment of students. This can add a new dimension to an assessment task. An example of this is if a student knows that an external expert will be watching their presentation, they may be more focused on making the content appropriate for them rather than an academic audience. Having an external expert taking part in a simulation rather than just other students adds more realism to the situation (Naylor et al., 2015). It has been identified that when external experts are involved in the assessment of clinical and patient care skills, they need training in providing constructive feedback (Hill et al., 2014). Although acknowledging they are external experts, some Turkish nursing students questioned whether service users had enough knowledge to make judgement on their clinical practice (Duygulu and Abaan, 2013). Others expressed concerns about a reduction in academic challenges impacting on academic quality (O'Donnell and Gormley, 2013). The evaluation by Muir and Laxton (2012) into the practice of external experts providing feedback on medical students' clinical assessment identified the importance of preparation and support for the external expert's involved. There was a danger that negative feedback might have a damaging effect on the student (O'Donnell and Gormley, 2013). Giving feedback is a skill that needs to be acquired and practised (Stacey et al., 2012). Thus, some form of training and support in providing constructive feedback is needed for a high-quality service (Hill et al., 2014). However, there is a fine line between addressing training and development needs and appearing patronising or placing unrealistic demands on the external expert (Gutteridge and Dobbins, 2010). To combat this, any training needs should be identified in partnership with them and tailored to their requirements. Students, particularly from mental health, expressed concern about the well-being of the external expert when participating in their education due to the potential vulnerability of the individual (O'Donnell and Gormley, 2013). This needs to be carefully managed.

Vignette
Involving external experts in the assessment of students can work well, but I learnt the value of effective briefing when one external expert took it upon themselves to make the task deliberately more difficult. Feedback to students from an external expert can be much more powerful than from an academic. For this to be successful they need training in giving feedback and be overseen by an academic.

Reflection
How can you involve external experts in the assessment of your students?
What preparation do you think both the students and the experts may need?

Involving external experts

Whilst this chapter has mainly focused on three areas of your curriculum – admissions, delivery, and assessment – external experts are also involved in other areas such as the quality of your programme covered in Chapter 3 and programme design and approval in Chapter 4. Consider how you can involve external experts across the life cycle of your students from recruitment to graduation.

Vignette
I have found that a passion for involving external expertise is needed to persevere through the logistical and organisational challenges encountered. At the start finding the right person to involve, and finding out if and how they should be paid or rewarded, was difficult. Arranging their involvement in terms of transport and room bookings needed consideration. On one occasion the room I had been allocated was in the depths of the university and challenging to access with a wheelchair. People-management skills are required to be able to effectively engage with the variety of expectations and personalities of the external experts. Some things are out of the control of a programme leader.

Reflection

- What support is available within your organisation in terms of involving external expertise?
- What system is in place to reward your external experts and how would you access this?
- What training do you and your delivery team need to successfully involve external experts?

Summary

This chapter has explored how you can enhance your students' experience through the introduction of external expertise. It identifies how external experts can contribute across the life cycle of your students and in doing so improve the quality of your programme. There are benefits to the students in terms of employability and benefits for the external experts such as in developing their curriculum vitae. There are challenges in engaging external expertise, and it takes organisation and management. You need to identify, recruit, and reward appropriate external experts. Both the external expert and students may need preparation and support to gain the most out of any interaction. Within this chapter, there is discussion around involvement in admissions, curriculum delivery, and assessment.

References

Ankrah, S. and Al-Tabbaa, O., 2015. Universities–industry collaboration: A systematic review. *Scandinavian Journal of Management*, 31(3), pp. 387–408.

Awasthy, R., Flint, S., Sankarnarayana, R., and Jones, R.L., 2020. A framework to improve university–industry collaboration. *Journal of Industry–University Collaboration*, 2(1), pp. 49–62.

Dowling, A., 2015. The Dowling review of business–university research collaborations. UK Government. Available from https://www.gov.uk/government/publications/business-university-research-collaborations-dowling-review-final-report (accessed 12 April 2022).

Duygulu, S. and Abaan, S., 2013. Turkish nursing students' views on practice assessments and service user involvement. *Contemporary Nurse*, 43(2), pp. 201–212.

Gutteridge, R. and Dobbins, K., 2010. Service user and carer involvement in learning and teaching: A faculty of health staff perspective. *Nurse Education Today*, 30(6), pp. 509–514.

Happell, B.et al., 2020. 'It is much more real when it comes from them': The role of experts by experience in the integration of mental health nursing theory and practice. *Perspectives in Psychiatric Care*, 56(4), pp. 811–819.

Health Education England, 2021. Values based recruitment. Available from https://www.hee.nhs.uk/our-work/values-based-recruitment (accessed 31 October 2021).

Hill, G., Thompson, G., Willis, S., and Hodgson, D., 2014. Embracing service user involvement in radiotherapy education: A discussion paper. *Radiography*, 20(1), pp. 82–86.

Lathlean, J., Burgess, A., Coldham, T., Gibson, C., Herbert, L., Levett-Jones, T., Simons, L., and Tee, S., 2006. Experiences of service user and carer participation in health care education. *Nurse Education Today*, 26(8), pp. 732–737.

Matka, E. River, D., Littlechild, R., and Powell, T., 2010. Involving service users and carers in admissions for courses in social work and clinical psychology: Cross-disciplinary comparison of practices at the University of Birmingham. *British Journal of Social Work*, 40(7), pp. 2137–2154.

Morisson, A. and Pattinson, M. (2020). *University–Industry Collaboration.* Interreg Europe Policy Learning Platform.

Muir, D. and Laxton, J.C., 2012. Experts by experience; the views of service user educators providing feedback on medical students' work based assessments. *Nurse Education Today*, 32(2), pp. 146–150.

Naylor, S., Harcus, J., and Elkington, M., 2015. *An exploration of service user involvement in the assessment of students. Radiography*, 21(3), pp. 269–272.

O'Donnell, H. and Gormley, K., 2013. Service user involvement in nurse education: Perceptions of mental health nursing students. *Journal of Psychiatric and Mental Health Nursing*, 20(3), pp. 193–202.

Quality Assurance Agency, 2018a. The revised UK Quality Code for Higher Education. Available from https://www.qaa.ac.uk/quality-code (accessed 31 October 2021).

Quality Assurance Agency, 2018b. UK Quality Code, Advice and Guidance: External Expertise. Available from https://www.qaa.ac.uk/quality-code/advice-and-guidance/external-expertise (accessed 31 October 2021).

Rakovska, N., Pavlin, S., and Melink, M., 2014. Assessment of cooperation between higher education institutions and employers in Europe. European Association of Institutions in Higher Education. Available from https://www.eurashe.eu/library/emcosu_assessment-of-cooperation-between-higher-education-institutions-and-employers-in-europe-wp4-report-pdf/last (accessed 24 September 2021).

Rhodes, C.A. and Nyawata, I.D., 2011. Service user and carer involvement in student nurse selection: Key stakeholder perspectives. *Nurse Education Today*, 31(5), pp. 439–443.

Sánchez, A., Domínguez, C., Blanco, J.M., and Jaime, A., 2019. Incorporating computing professionals' know-how: Differences between assessment by students, academics, and professional experts. *ACM Transactions on Computing Education (TOCE)*, 19(3), pp. 1–18.

Stacey, G., Stickley, T., and Rush, B., 2012. Service user involvement in the assessment of student nurses: A note of caution. *Nurse Education Today*, 5(32), pp. 482–484.

7 Work-based learning

Work-based learning

Work-based learning within the context of higher education is programmes where the higher education providers and work organisations jointly create learning opportunities (Boud and Solomon, 2003; QAA, 2018). Work-based learning provides an opportunity for students to explore careers, aids in the development of employability skills, and the transition to employment. Graduate employment has become a performance indicator (Higher Education Statistics Agency, 2021). Various studies have shown that work-based learning has a positive impact on graduate employment (Silva et al., 2018; Inceoglu et al., 2019). High Fliers (2021) report shows that, from those employers taking part in their study, an estimated 34 per cent of graduates recruited have had experience of work-based learning in their organisation, with many being given job offers at the end of their placement. Work-based learning can influence the student's attitude towards their programme, either by increasing motivation or by providing the realisation that the programme they are on is not leading them in the right direction (Inceoglu et al., 2019). Some students do leave a programme once they have experienced the reality of the work they are training for. Even a short period experiencing work-based learning can help students develop skills and assess their career direction (Thompson, 2017).

Virtual or e-internships were emerging before the start of the pandemic (Jeske and Axtell, 2014). These are learning experiences that are partially or fully computer-mediated, with supervisors, students, and their colleagues in different geographic locations. With recent changes in working practices due to the pandemic work-based learning for some students will radically change as working from home becomes the norm in some organisation. Virtual or e-placements have been used where other placement experience has been disrupted (Zuchowski et al., 2021). These can be any type of work experience that does not require the student to be physically located in the placement provider's premises. This raises issues around supervisor support, their working from home environment, and facilities. A qualitative study in Malaysia found that some companies provided students with items such as laptops,

DOI: 10.4324/9781003126355-8

whilst others did not (Ahmad, 2020). Whilst working from home can provide flexibility, save on costs, and help students prepare for future working practices, it does present challenges. They need to be carefully planned, have staff committed to supporting the students, and set out clear expectations (Jeske and Axtell, 2016).

David Boud has undertaken extensive research into learning in the workplace. He emphasises that learning from others at work is complex (Boud and Middleton, 2003). One thing that is difficult is being labelled a 'learner' or 'student' and not being accepted as a fully functioning member of the team which can cause discomfort in the workplace and set the student apart from the group (Boud and Solomon 2003; Newton and McKenna, 2007). However, the label 'student' can also be viewed as providing some protection from the full reality of practice. Social participation within the community is key to informal learning at work (Wenger 1999). Boud et al. (2009) stress the importance of talk, or more precisely chat, in the process of informal learning at work. There are spaces where learning takes place mainly through talking. The staffroom has been identified as a place where informal 'talk' can occur in a safe environment where hierarchy is suspended (Boud et al., 2009; Solomon et al., 2006). If the student is not accepted and welcomed into the environment experiencing marginalisation and isolation, they will not receive the support required.

Knowledge of the culture of the organisation will smooth the transition into the professional environment. Cultural knowledge is generally gained informally through social participation. As this knowledge is gained informally it is taken for granted because people are unaware of its influence on their behaviour (Eraut, 2007). Newton and McKenna (2007) identified the need to gain knowledge of social hierarchy and where a newcomer fits in. This knowledge is gained tacitly through a series of encounters which are generally set up for other purposes (Eraut, 1998, 2000). Some of Michael Eraut's early work looked at the development of professional knowledge and learning in the workplace (Eraut et al., 1998; Eraut 2000). He suggests that one of the most important features of the workplace is the people with whom one interacts such as colleagues and service users. If learning is viewed as a social act, then it involves relationships between people, the conversations and tasks that occur between them (Boud et al., 2009).

Different models of work-based learning are needed to meet the requirements of the variety of programmes (Costley and Armsby, 2007). This results in the terminology around work-based learning being varied and confusing. This can be problematic, particularly when negotiating with employers and other potential placement sites and aligning university and employer/placement expectations (Jackson et al., 2017). Here is a list of some of the common terms you may encounter:

Work-based learning: a period spent working in an organisation as part of a programme for students to gain practical training and experience.

Placement, work placement, or clinical placement: a period of supervised work that is spent as part of a programme to gain practical training and experience.
Work-integrated learning: work-related opportunities that take place during university studies.
Non-placement work-integrated learning: activities such as simulation and projects that connect students to authentic work-related learning.
Internships: a student working in an organisation, either with or without pay, to gain work experience or satisfy requirements for a qualification.
Practicums: practical training as part of a programme, aimed at helping students put theory into practice that lean more towards observation than experience.
Apprenticeships: programmes for people who are employed, working on the job while studying for a formal qualification.

Integrating learning

Work-based learning should be seen as an integrated part of the programme rather than something extra bolted on as this can become confusing for students (Costley and Armsby, 2007). Students need to see the value of their investment in work-based learning and make links between the different learning environments (Jackson, 2015). You can help your students view this as an integrated part of the programme by structuring educational intervention leading up to the placement, during the placement, and after. Students should understand what they are expected to learn, recognise if this learning has taken place, and identify future learning needs (Brodie and Irving, 2007). Much learning in the workplace occurs by being proactive and seeking out learning opportunities. This requires confidence as well as support, sometimes only moral support, from colleagues. Eraut (2000) suggested a triangular relationship between challenge, support, and confidence as factors that affect learning in the workplace. For students to progress their work they need to be challenged without being so daunted that it reduces their confidence (Eraut, 2007). Thus, a step-by-step approach to learning and development should smooth a student's journey. Vygotsky was a Russian psychologist well known to early years educators but whose teachings can be adapted to the learning and development of adults. His emphasis was on social interaction in learning, and he is known for his concept of the zone of proximal development, which explores the relationship between learning and development (Vygotsky and Cole, 1978). Contrary to the thinking of the time that learning was purely an external process, Vygotsky put forward the notion that learning and development are interrelated, and that learning takes the lead, rather than development, as previous philosophers thought (Vygotsky and Cole, 1978; Holzman, 2009). The zone of proximal development is the gap between what someone can do unaided and what they might do with support (Smidt 2009). This support may come in the form of an expert who helps the novice to take the steps to move from dependence to independence (Smidt, 2009). One term used to describe this support is scaffolding. This was introduced by psychologist Jerome Bruner (Fleer, 1990). Scaffolding in the form of support is gradually removed as mastery of the task is achieved (Smidt, 2009). Vygotsky suggested that a person can only imitate that which is within their development level (Vygotsky and Cole, 1978). Thus, learning and removal of support should be matched with the individual's development level (Vygotsky and Cole, 1978).

When, where, and how students gain work experience will be influenced by your university and the professional requirements for your programme. Students within your programme will all have individual requirements and as students will likely be spread across different work placements their experiences will vary. It is therefore challenging to facilitate an equitable experience for all students. As a programme leader, you should ensure that your students are well prepared for work-based learning. For some students, this will be their first experience in a workplace. They will be expected to act professionally, therefore, introducing them to what professionalism means to your particular discipline is beneficial (Kaufman and Ricci, 2014). They may need skills and knowledge before attending the workplace such as how they are expected to dress and communicate with the service users and other members of the workforce. Learners are more likely to reach their potential when they are supported by those with whom they share cultural tools, for example a common language (Smidt, 2009). Cultural differences between academia and the work placement are likely, which is an issue that may need addressing and for which students should be prepared (Reeve and Gallacher, 2005).

You can optimise the learning potential from a work placement by providing a platform for students to compare and critically discuss their experiences with each other (Billet et al., 2018). Reflection is an important aspect of learning through experience (Raelin, 2008; Jackson, 2015). Students should be introduced to these concepts alongside other academic skills to assist with the move towards learner-driven self-development (Rowe, 2019). Reflection, particularly for work-based learning, can be a social/collective process (Raelin, 2010). There are a variety of tools to aid reflection and self-development such as mentoring or peer mentoring, journals, logs, and workbooks (Clarke et al., 2018). You could consider encouraging students to write blogs, vlogs, or contribute to discussion boards because reflecting through dialogue can enhance learning for the students (Raelin, 2001).

Assessing work-based learning

In order to maximise the work-based learning experience, students should have clear learning objectives. Assessment activities should ideally be derived from real work, authentic activity (Jackson, 2015). Self- and peer assessment can help develop higher-level thinking around the practice of work (Costley and Armsby, 2007). It may be appropriate for employers to be involved in planning the learning and assessments. In some programmes, students will negotiate their own objectives for their work-based learning; for others linked to professional body recognition the learning objectives may be predetermined. Even within predetermined competencies or learning outcomes students should be encouraged to plan their learning and may need guiding into writing learning objectives that are specific, measurable, achievable, realistic, and timed (SMART) (Jackson, 2015). You should ensure your students have a good understanding of their learning objectives and how they can demonstrate that they have met these (Boud and Solomon, 2001).

A formal assessment of work-based learning can be challenging due to the complex interactions within the workplace (Benett, 1993). Students will experience different qualities within the learning environment and the supervision that they receive; this will hinder equity of assessment. When planning assessments, you should consider that the thought of being assessed during work-based learning can be quite daunting for a student, particularly if they are hoping to seek employment at that site once qualified. Some students put a lot of pressure on themselves which can be a cause of anxiety. A variety of assessment methods can be used to help students demonstrate their competency and that learning has taken place. These can be used individually or in combination. Many programmes require students to build a portfolio to capture and record a student's experience and learning. This can be used across a whole programme rather than linked to a specific module to help link theory to practice. It is an effective way of students being able to demonstrate that they meet learning outcomes and occupational standards. Other methods include the following:

- workbooks;
- patchwork assessment;
- learning journal/log;
- professional discussion;
- reflective reports;
- observations of practice;
- Work-based projects.

There should be a collaboration with placement providers when planning assessments about the processes, procedures, and documentation of assessment (Benett, 1993). There should also be discussion around the tasks and competencies most appropriate to assess and the potential for any bias. Some programmes require work-based supervisors to assess students. They can be well placed to comment on a student's performance from their day-to-day observation but will require training (Costley and Armsby, 2007; Jackson, 2015). Assessing and providing feedback is a skill in its self. Placement supervisors may be able to assess what a student can do but not the level of reasoning behind the skill (Costley and Armsby, 2007).

The work-based learning provider

Building positive relationships between the academic staff and the staff at the work placement is important as this helps issues to be dealt with promptly, before they escalate. It also helps the placement provider feeling well supported. Some universities may have a link tutor role. People within this role provide support for the placement staff, support students, and oversee their work-based learning (Kerridge, 2008). Effective communication facilitates consistency with the messages to students from both the university and practice learning facilitator. There is a benefit to three-way communication between the students, academic, and work placements, particularly regarding issues around attendance and punctuality. Communication mechanisms need to be flexible as placement staff may be busy and not be routinely accessing work emails. Some issues are best discussed face to face or via the telephone, although emails do provide an audit trail. Text messages can work in some instances; for example, for last-minute changes to arrangements. As programme leader, you could produce easily accessible information, such as short information video clips on a work-based learning website that contains information about the programme, copies of student's workbooks, and various documentation and guidance on what to do in different circumstances. You would need to continually signpost to this information as people in these roles will be constantly changing. One way is by adding a link to your email signature. New staff can start work in a workplace at any point in the year, demonstrating the need for a rolling programme for training staff who are supervising students with their work-based learning, or easily accessible information. Often staff learn how to mentor or supervise students from experience, their own or others which can lead to inconsistent practices. Arranging face-to-face courses is difficult, online material might be more accessible. Sometimes information will be cascaded to the supervising staff from a central person but this is not always a robust mechanism of communication as information can get diluted. Some universities provide their own credit-bearing awards for people facilitating work-based learning and some professional bodies have their own accreditation scheme (Minton and Lowe, 2019).

Larger organisations may employ people specifically as practice learning facilitators. They have a role in maintaining the quality of the learning experience and in building capacity for learning within their organization. A practice learning facilitator plays a critical role in helping students gain value from their experience. Another recognised role is the practice educator who has a role in teaching, supervising, and assessing students. They are the student-facing guides and mentors. There are demands on the time required for facilitating work-based learning, producing rosters for students, information for audits, and attending meetings at the university. Sometimes these result in demands on their time that conflicts with their other job roles (Minton and Lowe, 2019). The requirements of the role increases as student numbers increase and become more time-consuming. Sometimes the practice educator or facilitator is a dedicated role, but this is not always the case. Sometimes it is a member of staff who takes an interest in students and fits facilitating students' learning around their other roles. There should be formal support for workplace facilitators (Minton and Lowe, 2019). According to Boud et al. (2009), the intervention by managers can enhance learning in the workplace. Therefore, managerial support is required for anyone supporting students undertaking work-based learning. There needs to be a close relationship with employers to provide a holistic approach to learning (Minton and Lowe, 2019), one that meets the needs of the student and employer/placement provider (Rowe, 2019).

There are actions you can take as programme leader to support the practice learning facilitator/practice educator. You should ensure there are clear guidelines about the roles, responsibilities, and expectations of the practice learning facilitator and/or practice educator. The time dedicated to these roles should be considered, particularly when looking to increase student capacity in a workplace area. Time and guidance are essential, particularly for anyone new to the role. If you can arrange for people responsible for the student experience from different places of work to meet together it provides a positive platform for sharing ideas and experiences. Other suggestions include:

- informal meetings in the workplace;
- joint induction for students and facilitators/practice educators;
- a facilitator/practice educator handbook.

(Minton and Lowe, 2019)

Managing the student experience

One of the strengths of work-based learning is its flexible and negotiated nature of learning, but this can also present a challenge. It provides a problem for some learners as they lack the scaffolding and structure experienced in other modules. Supporting the move towards independent learning is important. You will need to have mechanisms in place to support and oversee your student's experience. Throughout their programme, but particularly when a student is on placement, we want students to take ownership of their learning and therefore need to develop a coaching approach, allowing them to take responsibility. Various models are available including the competency-based Synergy model (Curley, 2007), the Collaborative Learning in Practice (CLiP) model (Lobo et al., 2014; Clarke et al., 2018), and peer learning. These set the tone for how students are in charge of their learning, rather than a teacher-led approach. Gibson and Busby (2009) found through conducting focus groups with undergraduate students that students do not think support is important until something goes wrong. Sometimes intervention will be required and students should know where to go for support with different issues that may arise. These include how to report any sickness and absence, whom to approach, and what to do if they have an adverse experience during their work-based learning, and where to go if they have a problem or are struggling.

Preparation before starting a work placement is important (Jackson, 2015). Students may have anxieties before starting work-based learning. They may find themselves working in different cultural environments and preparation will help alleviate stresses about meeting expectations of the work placement. If not already familiar with a work placement, and if practical, it is useful for students to have a pre-placement visit to ensure that they know where to go on the first day, how to get there, and whom to ask for. It is nice if they can meet and greet the person who will be supervising them before starting the work-based learning. Another valuable preparation of the students is if they can chat with other students who have attended the same placement. It may not be feasible for students to do a pre-placement site visit. If this is the case they could arrange a video call with a member of staff at the placement site. Some work placements have used GoPros to film work areas so students get a feel for the layout they are about to enter. These strategies all help to reduce anxieties as students can gain practical information as well as an awareness of what to expect. Practical manuals or work-based learning handbooks can be a useful source of information. These can be informed by and co-designed with students who have previously attended the same placement.

Students engaging in work-based learning, particularly if geographically remote from the university, can feel isolated. The time pressures of work and study may impact keeping in touch with friends, family, and the university (Gibson and Busby, 2009). Focus groups with student nurses, a professional programme with a high proportion of clinical placement, identified that some students feel abandoned when moving from university to their clinical placement (Brown et al., 2004). Different strategies have been explored to reduce this isolation. To help address the challenge of isolation, students in Ireland were required to engage with a peer group blog assessment. This encouraged students to reflect and initiate peer-to-peer learning with the facility for students to comment on each other's blogs (Dunne and Ryan, 2016). Student support can also be addressed if they are visited by a representative from the university whilst on placement (Gibson and Busby, 2009). If face-to-face visits are not practical, virtual visits may be equally effective in reducing the feelings of abandonment.

International students and students undertaking international placements may need additional support in adjusting to the culture in the workplace (Attrill et al., 2020). This could be facilitated by engaging in discussion about cultural values and helping students to develop effective relationships at their placement site (Attrill et al., 2020). Similarly, a student with placements abroad will also need special consideration (Conroy and McCarthy, 2019).

Support can be broken down into three areas, pre-departure, arrival, and repatriation (Conroy and McCarthy, 2019). Whilst these three areas have specific issues when students have placements abroad, there are also occasions whereby support can be tailored for all students experiencing work-based learning. An action research study with business students on an international placement identified themes of professional, cultural, and personal adjustment (Conroy and McCarthy, 2019). Various strategies can be used to alleviate these challenges. These include using technology to facilitate continued support and communication from the university. However, technology such as telephone and internet connections may be problematic in some areas (Gibson and Bushby, 2009). On returning to university students can struggle to adjust back into the university environment. This is a consideration for all students, not just from international placements and they may experience feelings of anxiety at returning to university study. Facilitating a debrief and reflection will help students to process their experience and apply the practice to theory and vice versa.

Struggling students

Struggling students can take up a lot of your time as programme leader. Early identification will enable timely intervention to support these students. To be able to do this we need to understand our students. Failure has emotional and financial implications for the student, and an apprentice on a degree programme may lose their job. In the current education climate of programmes being judged by metrics such as graduate employment, it has implications for your programme. Whilst not probing too much into personal details it is useful to understand any financial, practical, or emotional factors that may impact on a student succeeding at their work-based learning (Davenport, et al., 2018).

The critical narrative review by Davenport et al. (2018) raised the concept of 'failure to fail'. This is where marginal, struggling students pass and continue to struggle, eventually becoming weak practitioners. This is often due to the complex interaction between the practice educators and students. Practice educators, either from a personal connection with the student or lack of confidence feel pressure to pass a student. It is therefore important to support both the struggling student and the practice educator. Students can struggle with work-based learning for all sorts of different reasons. These can be broken down into short-term issues and longer-term problems. Some issues can easily be addressed whilst other problems may take time to adjust. Students may struggle for practical reasons such as travel, money, or accommodation. They struggle for emotional reasons like bereavement and homesickness. Some issues can be social, where students struggle to adjust to the cultural differences in the work-based placement. It may also be the case that a practice educator considers a student is struggling, but the student does not recognise this.

Poor timekeeping, attendance, and absence reporting are the most frequently raised issues by work-based learning providers. If this is a student's first exposure to working, or they do not have a background where attendance and punctuality are valued they may not recognise that there is a problem with their behaviour. With any issue, early identification and remedial action planning is key to success. One way to do this is to raise a cause for concern. This is a supportive mechanism, rather than disciplinary, and the supportive nature of this process should be stressed with the student. An example process can be seen in the flow chart in Figure 7.1. The important point to note about this process is that it is open and transparent; discussions are a three-way process involving the student, practice educator, and link academic tutor. Meetings should be clearly documented with facts, not opinions; an action plan should be put in place documenting actions for the student, placement provider, and link academic tutor, and a date for a follow-up meeting set.

Failing students

For some students, work-based learning will mainly be about gaining experience; for others, it will be an integral, assessed part of the programme. It may be essential to pass their work-based learning to progress or complete the programme. Failure is not a term that is used comfortably and failing a student on their work-based learning can be particularly challenging. However,

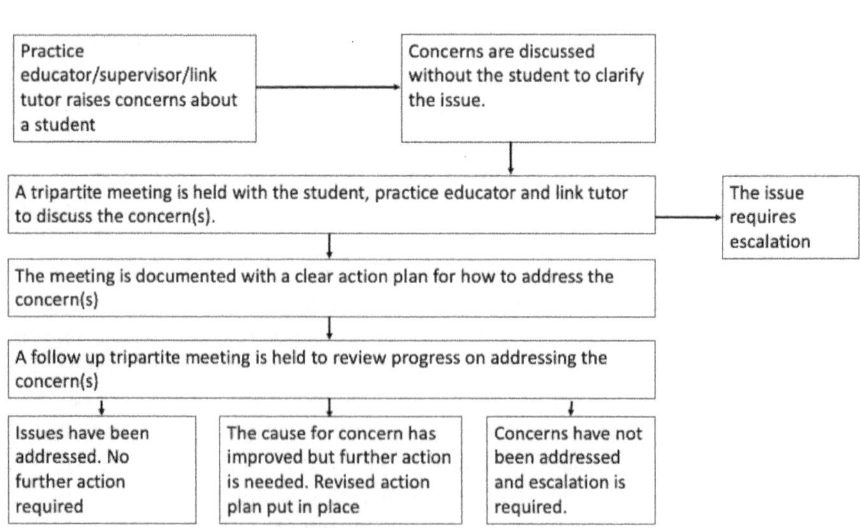

Figure 7.1 The cause for concern process

the practice educator evaluating student competence is the gatekeeper of their profession (Finch, 2017). In some programmes it is a matter of protecting public safety. In these cases, expectations should be clarified from the outset so students appreciate the role of a work-based learning assessment within their programme.

Managing quality

As programme leader, you should consider the equality for students accessing work-based learning. Student characteristics such as background, ethnicity, and gender can all have an impact (Binder et al., 2015). The QAA and professional and regulatory bodies oversee the quality of a work placement. As a programme leader, some of the actions that you can take to enhance quality are followed.

- Ensure that each student has an identified personal academic tutor who can oversee their learning experience.
- Collect feedback regularly from learners to help enhance your programme.
- Record and action plan to address any issues raised regarding placement.
- Have in place a system to regularly review and to document a student's progress.
- Ensure regular contact with practice learning facilitators, placement supervisors, or mentors and a mechanism for them to provide feedback.

Monitoring the quality of placement should be undertaken at relevant time points throughout the academic year (Jackson et al., 2017). There are various ways of monitoring the student experience including canvasing the students' opinion through anonymous electronic polling. The anonymity means that students can give an honest opinion without fear of reprisals. Any feedback from students should be shared with a placement area. In addition, feedback needs to be gathered from the placement to gauge perception of the students' experience. Auditing the placement area can be formal or informal depending on the requirements of the programme. Some programmes may need to adhere to external professional or regulatory bodies. Potential areas that may be covered include:

- the learning environment such as staff to student ratio;
- governance and leadership arrangements;
- facilities for supporting learners;
- support and training for practice educators and supervisors.

As well as auditing the direct work placement, it may be necessary to undertake a higher-level organisational audit. Audits should be undertaken in conjunction with the placement provider resulting in a documented action plan. Action must be taken if a placement area is falling below the required standard. In extreme cases, a student may need to be removed from their placement until the situation improves.

Ideally, there should be a memorandum of understanding between the placement provider and the university. This can be tailored depending on the nature of your programme. A bipartite agreement outlines expectations, behaviours, and actions of the placement provider and the university. Some programmes that are professionally regulated will require partnership agreements that are reviewed and agreed upon by the university legal team. Work placements may have students from different universities. In this case, it is advisory to have an additional tripartite agreement between the provider and both universities thus ensuring understanding between all three parties.

In addition to the organisation partnership agreement. For the student undertaking work-based learning there may also be an individual partnership agreement between the student, placement, and the university. This is useful to clarify the expectations and responsibilities of each party. This can take the form of a learning contract, as in the example below:

The placement has a right to expect students to:

1 behave in a professional and respectful manner;
2 proactively engage in their learning;
3 be punctual and reliable;
4 to effectively communicate any absences;
5 be flexible in their engagement with learning opportunities.

The placement has a right to expect the university to provide:

1 timely information about students attending the placement;
2 regular up-to-date information about policies and processes;
3 information and support regarding student assessments.

Students have the right to expect

1 courtesy and respect;
2 to be treated as a valued member of the placement;
3 the opportunity to gain relevant experience;
4 have a safe supportive environment.

The university staff have the right to expect:

1 placements and students to engage with quality assurance processes;
2 opportunity to meet with placement staff and students;
3 placement staff and students to engage in effective communication.

Students may be exposed to poor standards of practice or working habits (Jackson, 2015; Minton and Lowe, 2019). They may be unhappy with their placement and feel exploited in some way (Gibson and Busby, 2009). Sometimes incidents may happen on a placement that is of a serious or untoward nature such as sexual harassment (Emslie, 2009). There should be an effective process for reporting and investigating these. Students may be reluctant to raise a concern or report an incident and should be supported through this process. There need to be clear lines of communication and a transparent process. Work placements will likely have their own policies and procedures to follow as well as those provided by the university. A procedure should be in place for a student to disclose information about the conduct of another individual. Whistleblowing under any circumstances is difficult but it is important that students are able to raise concerns about staff from the university, placement, or other students.

Vignette

As a programme leader, I have come across some tricky situations to deal with. One which is memorable due to its complexity is a student who was sexually harassed on placement. She approached me a few weeks after the incident having tried to deal with the situation herself. As with many cases of this nature, it was not overt, but subtle, leading her to question what she had heard and trying to dismiss the incident. The year-one student was a school leaver in her first placement. The actions I took were threefold:

(I) referred the student to student well-being so that she had the opportunity for mental well-being support.

(II) raised the matter with the practice learning facilitator who informed me that the person in question was renowned for his lewd comments. However, just because some people ignore or accept this behaviour does not make it right.

(III) The incident was discussed with the manager of the placement. They took the matter further through their organisation's human resources processes.

After some time I had another meeting with the student who whilst concerned about going back to the placement was reassured that her concerns had been taken seriously. Further support was provided by the practice learning facilitator. It was good that this student felt able to disclose their situation. Harassment is not always of a sexual nature and there are many reasons why a student may not disclose incidents of harassment. They may be concerned about remaining on placement after making a complaint for fear of victimisation, being labelled a trouble maker. They may worry about being seen as unable to cope, or being incompetent. This may lead to concerns about the impact of disclosure on their grade. Students have a right to be treated with respect and learn in a safe environment universities have a responsibility to prepare graduates with the skills to prevent and respond to harassment. There should be transparency in how universities respond to incidents of harassment.

Emslie (2009) provides a model from youth-work education aiming to prepare students and supporting staff in preventing and responding to sexual harassment on placement. The following points have been adapted from this model:

- Have robust organisational policies and a clear statement that harassment will be taken seriously
- Have online resources for staff and students that help identify harassment and provide a guide on what to do when harassment takes place.
- Include harassment as part of the curriculum, facilitating open discussion and material to equip students before they start their placement.
- Offer professional development to placement providers.
- Consult with other agencies to ensure policies and processes are up to date.
- Develop quality tripartite relationships between students, academics, and placement providers to facilitate a safe, supportive learning environment.
- Have a student-centred approach to any incidents and encourage a student in the use of their own coping strategies.
- Ensure that people involved in facilitating work-based education are effectively recognised and adequately resourced.
- Consider environmental factors that contribute to harassment. Look at what policies are in place in the work-based learning environment.
- Continually monitor and review policies and processes ensuring they are current and fit for purpose.

Reflection

Considering the points above. What do you have in place to identify, prevent, and respond to harassment in your work-based learning environments?

The health and safety of students on work placements is clearly important. The provider of placement should give assurance around how they provide a safe environment and manage risks. A risk assessment should be carried out for each placement site and some students with individual needs will require a personalised risk assessment. If a student sources their own placement they should ensure that a risk assessment has been undertaken. Students should be fully aware of any risk involved before attending placement. They have a responsibility to manage their own risk whilst on placement. How to do this forms an important part of pre-placement preparation. How, for example, liability and travel insurance are covered should be clarified before a student attends placement. You should consider refusing to approve a placement if you consider that health and safety are not being effectively managed. Aspects to consider include:

- The environment
- Lone or remote working
- Travel arrangements
- Accommodation
- Access to medical services
- Individual student factors

It is useful to have guides available to students for a variety of aspects including safe travel, dress code, remote working, and safe use of social media.

Apprenticeships

Changes in the funding stream in the UK have seen an increase in apprenticeships particularly degree apprenticeships (Rowe et al., 2016). With apprenticeships rather than the higher education institute having a contract with a workplace to provide a placement, an employer contracts a university to provide a programme, putting the employer firmly in control of the education and training that they require. You may be a programme leader of an apprenticeship degree. Work-based or work-integrated learning is the main focus of any apprenticeship. It is viewed that they are an employee first and a student second (ASET, 2019). The formal agreements between the education provider and employer will be different to higher education students on an unpaid work placement. However, as programme leader, your role will be to facilitate the development of their learning, knowledge, skills, and behaviours as with any student. This can be achieved by working with the employer and recognising the apprentice's individual curriculum needs, providing stretch, and challenging appropriately. The entry into the programme and formal contracts with the work placement will be different. Essentially employers are in the driving seat; the majority of the apprentice's time will be on-the-job training with a minimum of 20 per cent off-the-job training. A typical attendance model is day release or block teaching. There can be blended learning with a few synchronous sessions, but not pure asynchronous distance learning. From the student's perspective, they do not pay for their training and are not eligible for student loans (Rowe et al., 2016). The university programme must conform to the relevant apprenticeship standard developed by a trailblazer. The apprenticeship standards describe the knowledge, skills, and behaviours (KSBs) that the apprentice should develop by the end of the programme. These form the content of the curriculum for the programme. In addition to the quality assurance agency, OFSTED will also inspect the quality of higher apprenticeship training. Apprentices will require personalised learning and authentic assessment (ASET, 2019). Assessments must be linked to the KSBs of the standard, and authentic real work activities used for assessment purposes. In the UK the Institute for Apprenticeships and Technical Education (IfATE) must approve the assessment plan and the endpoint assessment arrangements. Apprenticeships are employer-led and throughout the apprenticeship the university must work very closely with each employer. This means that you as programme leader must develop and maintain good relationships with an employer.

Recommendations for your degree apprenticeships include:

- designing programmes to meet the needs of the employer rather than adapting or combining with existing programmes;
- working with the employer on the delivery model;
- regularly reviewing your programme with relevant stakeholders;
- using assessment methods that reflect the workplace practice;

- involving employers in the design of assessments;
- developing the reflective practice of your students.(Rowe, 2019)

Summary

This chapter has explored work-based learning. Most programmes will provide students with the opportunity to learn from an authentic work experience. This enables students to explore careers, aids in the development of employability skills, and the transition to employment. There are different modes of work-based learning and various terminology used in association with providing students with this experience of integrating theory with practice. Programme leaders have a role in ensuring students are prepared for their placement and have the opportunity to reflect and learn from their experience. Assessments should be devised in collaboration with the placement provider to ensure they are authentic and linked to learning objectives. Programme leaders have a role in building positive relationships with placement providers and supporting those facilitating work-based learning. It is important to manage the process and quality of the student experience. The chapter covers strategies for identifying and supporting struggling students and discusses failing students. Degree apprenticeships are increasing and the final section in this chapter has provided a short overview of these.

Reflection

Here are some top tips to optimise a student's work-based learning. Think about your own programme and consider how you facilitate the following points.

How do you ensure that your students see the value of work experience?
Do your students have defined learning objectives before starting placement and do these consider students' preferences?
Scaffolding helps the students to mature and make informed decisions about their career path so ideally placements should start early in the educational process not be left until the last year. How do you structure work experience in your programme?
Consider the authenticity of the placement. Does this replicate expectations that employers may have in the future?
How do you support continuous communication between the student and their supervisor?
How do you help students apply theory into practice?
Reflective practice is essential in helping students to identify their own professional development. How do you encourage students to be reflective?

References

Ahmad, N.N., 2020. Accounting students' internship satisfaction on the work from home (WFH) experience during internship. *Global Business & Management Research*, 12(4), pp. 12–23.

ASET, 2019. ASET good practice guide to successful work based learning for apprenticeships in higher education. Available from https://www.asetonline.org/wp-content/

uploads/2019/06/ASET-Good-Practice-Guide-to-Successful-Work-Based-Learning-for-Apprenticeships-in-Higher-Education.pdf (accessed 15 November 2021).

Attrill, S., Lincoln, M., and McAllister, S., 2020. International students in professional placements: Supervision strategies for positive learning experiences. *International Journal of Language & Communication Disorders*, 55(2), pp. 243–254.

Benett, Y., 1993. The validity and reliability of assessments and self-assessments of work-based learning. *Assessment & Evaluation in Higher Education*, 18(2), pp. 83–94.

Billett, S., Cain, M., and Le, A.H., 2018. Augmenting higher education students' work experiences: Preferred purposes and processes. *Studies in Higher Education*, 43(7), pp. 1279–1294.

Binder, J.F., Baguley, T., Crook, C., and Miller, F., 2015. The academic value of internships: Benefits across disciplines and student backgrounds. *Contemporary Educational Psychology*, 41, pp. 73–82.

Boud, D. and Middleton, H. (2003). Learning from others at work: Communities of practice and informal learning. Journal of Workplace Learning, 15(5), pp. 194–202.

Boud, D., Rooney, D., and Solomon, N. (2009). Talking up learning at work: Cautionary tales in co-opting everyday learning. *International Journal of Lifelong Education*, 28(3), 323–334.

Boud, D. and Solomon, N. (2001) *Work-based learning: a new higher education?* Open University Press.

Boud, D. and Solomon, N. (2003). 'I don't think I am a learner': Acts of naming learners at work. *Journal of Workplace Learning*, 15(7), pp. 326–331.

Brodie, P. and Irving, K., 2007. Assessment in work-based learning: investigating a pedagogical approach to enhance student learning. *Assessment & Evaluation in Higher Education*, 32(1), pp. 11–19.

Brown, L., Herd, K., Humphries, G., and Paton, M., 2005. The role of the lecturer in practice placements: what do students think? *Nurse Education in Practice*, 5(2), pp. 84–90.

Clarke, D., Williamson, G.R., and Kane, A., 2018. Could students' experiences of clinical placements be enhanced by implementing a Collaborative Learning in Practice (CliP) model? *Nurse Education in Practice*, November 33, A3–A5. doi:10.1016/j.nepr.2018.03.002.

Conroy, K.M. and McCarthy, L., 2019. Abroad but not abandoned: Supporting student adjustment in the international placement journey. *Studies in Higher Education*, 46(6), pp. 1175–1189.

Costley, C. and Armsby, P., 2007. Work-based learning assessed as a field or a mode of study. *Assessment & Evaluation in Higher Education*, 32(1), pp. 21–33.

Curley, M.A., 2007. *Synergy: The unique relationship between nurses and patients, the AACN Synergy model for patient care.* Sigma Theta Tau.

Davenport, R., Hewat, S., Ferguson, A., McAllister, S., and Lincoln, M., 2018. Struggle and failure on clinical placement: A critical narrative review. *International Journal of Language & Communication Disorders*, 53(2), pp. 218–227.

Dunne, J. and Ryan, S.M., 2016. Enhancing professional development and supporting students on work-placement by peer-peer learning using an online reflective blog assessment. *Irish Journal of Academic Practice*, 5(1). doi:10.21427/D7HT51.

Emslie, M., 2009. Supporting students who are sexually harassed on placement. *The Journal of Practice Teaching and Learning*, 9(3), pp. 6–25.

Eraut, M., 1998. Concepts of competence. *Journal of Interprofessional Care*, 12(2), pp. 127–139.

Eraut, M., 2000. Non-formal learning and tacit knowledge in professional work. *British Journal of Educational Psychology*, 70(1), pp. 113–136.

Eraut, M., 2007. Learning from other people in the workplace. *Oxford Review of Education*, 33(4), pp. 403–422.

Finch, J., 2017. *Supporting struggling students on placement: A practical guide.* Policy Press.

Fleer, Marilyn, 1990. Scaffolding conceptual change in early childhood. *Research in Science Education*, 20(1), pp. 114–123.

Gibson, P. and Busby, G., 2009. Experiencing work: Supporting the undergraduate hospitality, tourism and cruise management student on an overseas work placement. *Journal of Vocational Education and Training*, 61(4), pp. 467–480.

Higher Education Statistics Agency, 2021. Graduate outcomes. Available from https://www.graduateoutcomes.ac.uk/ (accessed 12 November 2021).

High Fliers, 2021. The graduate market in 2021. Available from https://www.highfliers.co.uk/download/2021/graduate_market/GM21-Report.pdf (accessed 15 November 2021).

Holzman, L. (2009). *Vygotsky at work and play.* Routledge.

Inceoglu, I., Selenko, E., McDowall, A., and Schlachter, S., 2019. (How) Do work placements work? Scrutinizing the quantitative evidence for a theory-driven future research agenda. *Journal of Vocational Behavior*, 110, pp. 317–337.

Jackson, D., 2015. Employability skill development in work-integrated learning: Barriers and best practice. *Studies in Higher Education*, 40(2), pp. 350–367.

Jackson, D., Rowbottom, D., Ferns, S., and McLaren, D., 2017. Employer understanding of work-integrated learning and the challenges of engaging in work placement opportunities. *Studies in Continuing Education*, 39(1), pp. 35–51.

Jeske, D. and Axtell, C., 2014. e-Internships: Prevalence, characteristics and role of student perspectives. *Internet Research*.

Jeske, D. and Axtell, C.M., 2016. How to run successful e-internships: a case for organizational learning. *Development and Learning in Organizations: An International Journal*, 24(4), pp. 457–473.

Kaufman, T.J. and Ricci, P., 2014. Creation of a professionalism scale for hospitality students: an exploratory study. *SAGE Open*, 4(4), 2158244014559016.

Kerridge, J.L., 2008. Supporting student nurses on placement in nursing homes: The challenges for the link-tutor role. *Nurse Education in Practice*, 8(6), pp. 389–396.

Lobo, C., Arthur, A., and Lattimer, V., 2014. Collaborative Learning in Practice (CLiP) for pre-registration nursing students. *University of East England.*

Minton, A. and Lowe, J., 2019. How are universities supporting employers to facilitate effective "on the job" learning for apprentices? *Higher Education, Skills and Work-Based Learning*, 9(2), pp. 200–210.

Newton, J.M. and McKenna, L., 2007. The transitional journey through the graduate year: A focus group study. *International Journal of Nursing Studies*, 44(7), pp. 1231–1237.

Quality Assurance Agency. 2018. UK Quality Code, Advice and Guidance: Work-based Learning. Available https://www.qaa.ac.uk/quality-code/subject-benchmark-statements/advice-and-guidance/work-based-learning (accessed 12 November 2021).

Raelin, J.A., 2001. Public reflection as the basis of learning. *Management Learning*, 32 (1), pp. 11–30.

Raelin, J.A., 2008. *Work-based learning: Bridging knowledge and action in the workplace.* New and revised edn. Jossey-Bass.

Raelin, J.A., 2010. Work-based learning: Valuing practice as an educational event. *New Directions for Teaching and Learning*, 2010(124), pp. 39–46.

Reeve, F. and Gallacher, J., 2005. Employer–university 'partnerships': a key problem for work-based learning programmes? *Journal of Education and Work*, 18(2), pp. 219–233.

Rowe, L., 2019. Educating for the modern world: A report review. *Journal of Work-Applied Management*.

Rowe, L., Perrin, D., and Wall, T., 2016. The chartered manager degree apprenticeship: trials and tribulations. *Higher Education, Skills and Work-Based Learning*, 11(1), pp. 5–16.

Silva, P., Lopes, B., Costa, M., Melo, A.I., Dias, G.P., Brito, E., and Seabra, D., 2018. The million-dollar question: can internships boost employment? *Studies in Higher Education*, 43(1), pp. 2–21.

Smidt, Sandra (2009). *Introducing Vygotsky: A guide for practitioners and students in the early years.* Routledge.

Solomon, N., Boud, D., and Rooney, D., 2006. The in-between: Exposing everyday learning at work. *International Journal of Lifelong Education*, 25(1), pp. 3–13.

Thompson, D.W., 2017. How valuable is 'short project' placement experience to higher education students? *Journal of Further and Higher Education*, 41(3), pp. 413–424.

Vygotsky, L.S. and Cole, M. (1978). *Mind in society: The development of higher psychological processes.* Harvard University Press.

Wenger, E., 1999. *Communities of practice: Learning, meaning, and identity.* Cambridge University Press.

Zuchowski, I., Collingwood, H., Croaker, S., Bentley-Davey, J., Grentell, M., and Rytkönen, F., 2021. Social work e-placements during COVID-19: Learnings of staff and students. *Australian Social Work*, 74(3), pp. 373–386.

Conclusion

In this conclusion, I offer some final comments about being an effective programme leader.

Being an effective programme leader requires leadership skills. There are several approaches to leadership and you may have a preferred style. However, different styles of leadership are required in different situations. You may not feel that you have all the skills required to be an effective programme leader, but these will develop over time. You will need skills in motivating, networking, building collegiality, and dealing with difficult situations and people.

You are likely to be juggling programme leadership alongside other roles. To be an effective programme leader you should have a clear understanding of the requirements of the programme leader role. This is challenging because it changes both within and between universities. Peer support will help you thrive in this role. Being able to share experiences and learn from others is extremely useful. Alongside this is learning from more experienced programme leaders. Mentoring has a long history and can be very beneficial as you develop as a programme leader. The pressure experienced by programme leaders can be immense. Being aware of workplace stress and strategies for alleviating this will help you thrive in the role.

As programme leader, you are accountable for the quality of your programme. It is useful to understand the history and drivers for quality within higher education. This chapter introduces concepts related to engaging with students and other stakeholders for monitoring and reviewing your programme. It also covers some of the skills you will need including organising and chairing meetings, mechanisms for gathering feedback and improving the quality of your programme.

You may have taken over an established programme or be designing a new one. Chapter 4 explores programme design and approval. It details the processes involved and some of the key topics including co-creation of the curriculum, education for sustainable development, and internationalising the curriculum. There are many tools and techniques for quality and service improvement. Ones that have been used previously for programme design have been included such as nominal group and Delphi techniques.

Student experience should be high on the agenda of any programme leader. Chapter 5 is dedicated to this topic. It starts by exploring the important issue of

DOI: 10.4324/9781003126355-9

mental well-being and covers how a programme leader can support the mental well-being of students. It also covers specific interventions that you can use such as personal tutoring, peer tutoring, and peer mentoring. The transition onto your programme can be a particularly difficult time for students. Key actions that you can take to help students have a positive experience at different stages throughout the transition period are discussed. The chapter finishes by looking at some of the wider issues relating to student experience in higher education. These include equality, diversity and inclusion, and decolonisation. Information about using analytics to support your students' experience is also included.

Involving external expertise in the delivery of your programme can have many benefits in terms of students' satisfaction and employability skills. Advantages and barriers to involving external experts are discussed and information about how to effectively organise their involvement is provided. External expert involved is discussed at different stages in the student life cycle including admissions, curriculum delivery, and assessment.

The last chapter explores the topic of work-based learning. There is likely to be some element of work-based learning included in your programme. This chapter looks at the concept of work-based learning, how this can be integrated as part of a programme, and assessed. It looks at the relationship with the work-based learning provider and how positive relationships can be fostered. Managing the student experience whilst they are engaged in work-based learning presents some challenges. The chapter includes a discussion about overcoming these, particularly around students who are struggling. With changes in funding streams, there is a rise in degree apprenticeships. Therefore, a discussion about these has been included.

Vignettes have been included throughout this book. These can be used as a way of learning from the experiences of others and prompt you to reflect on your practice. Questions and scenarios have also been included to help you think critically and reflect on how you can be an effective programme leader.

This book can be used to develop your professional practice. An important element to this is action planning. Smart action planning will help you achieve your goals. Try to make your actions very specific, with a clear focus that is manageable and realistic. If you set a timeframe for any actions they are more likely to be achieved. Think beforehand about how you will measure or recognise that you have achieved your goals. Seeing the fruits of your actions will help you to have a sense of achievement.

It was my aim in writing this book that I could produce something that would help and support programme leaders. I hope that you have found something within its contents that is useful, informative, or valuable to you.

Index

Page numbers in *italics* indicate illustrations, **bold** a table

Lightning Source UK Ltd.
Milton Keynes UK
UKHW020617191122
412402UK00024B/451